The Critical Idiom

Founder Editor: JOHN D. JUMP (1969–1976)

13 Irony

DISCARDED
Fordham University Librarie

Irony / D. C. Muecke

Methuen & Co Ltd

Fordham University
LIBRARY
AT
LINCOLN CENTER
New York, N. Y.

BH
301
I7m8
cp.3

First published 1970
Reprinted 1973 and 1976
by Methuen & Co Ltd
11 New Fetter Lane, London EC4P 4EE
Reprinted 1978

© 1970 D. C. Muecke

Printed in Great Britain
by J. W. Arrowsmith Ltd, Bristol

ISBN 0 416 65420 7

*This paperback edition is sold subject to the condition
that it shall not by way of trade or otherwise, be lent, resold,
hired out, or otherwise circulated without the publisher's prior
consent in any form of binding or cover other than
that in which it is published and without a similar
condition including this condition being imposed
on the subsequent purchaser.*

Distributed in the U.S.A. by
HARPER & ROW PUBLISHERS, INC.
BARNES & NOBLE IMPORT DIVISION

Contents

General Editor's Preface

The volumes composing the Critical Idiom deal with a wide variety of key terms in our critical vocabulary. The purpose of the series differs from that served by the standard glossaries of literary terms. Many terms are adequately defined for the needs of students by the brief entries in these glossaries, and such terms do not call for attention in the present series. But there are other terms which cannot be made familiar by means of compact definitions. Students need to grow accustomed to them through simple and straightforward but reasonably full discussions. The main purpose of this series is to provide such discussions.

Many critics have borrowed methods and criteria from currently influential bodies of knowledge or belief that have developed without particular reference to literature. In our own century, some of them have drawn on art-history, psychology, or sociology. Others, strong in a comprehensive faith, have looked at literature and literary criticism from a Marxist or a Christian or some other sharply defined point of view. The result has been the importation into literary criticism of terms from the vocabularies of these sciences and creeds. Discussions of such bodies of knowledge and belief in their bearing upon literature and literary criticism form a natural extension of the initial aim of the Critical Idiom.

Because of their diversity of subject-matter, the studies in the series vary considerably in structure. But all authors have tried to give as full illustrative quotation as possible, to make reference whenever appropriate to more than one literature, and to write in such a way as to guide readers towards the short bibliographies in which they have made suggestions for further reading.

John D. Jump

University of Manchester

Acknowledgements

The following permissions to quote from published works are acknowledged:

From *The Poetry and Prose of Heinrich Heine*, edited by Frederic Ewen. Copyright, 1948, by the Citadel Press, Inc.

From *Nineteenth Century German Tales*, edited by Angel Flores. Copyright © 1959 by Angel Flores. Reprinted by permission of Professor Angel Flores and Doubleday & Company, Inc.

From *Waiting for Godot* and *Endgame* by Samuel Beckett. Reprinted by permission of Faber & Faber and Grove Press, Inc.

From *Electra and other plays* by Sophocles, translated by E. F. Watling. Reprinted by permission of Penguin Books Ltd.

From *The Man Without Qualities* by Robert Musil, translated by Eithne Wilkins and Ernst Kaiser. Reprinted by permission of Martin Secker & Warburg Ltd. and Franz J. Horch Associates, Inc.

From *Of Irony, Especially in Drama*, by G. G. Sedgewick. Copyright, Canada, 1935, 1948, by University of Toronto Press and London: Oxford University Press.

I

Introduction

The questions one asks concerning irony are these: What is it? What forms does it take, and how are these related to one another? What makes people ironical? What are the functions and uses of irony? How important is it? What is its history? Is it found in all cultures? Is there no sin in it?

This work undertakes to say something in answer to most of these questions. Given the notorious elusiveness of the concept of irony, it will be a principal task to identify the common properties or constituent factors of irony, and we shall spend some time in distinguishing and illustrating the chief forms that irony takes. It will not do, however, to give the impression that these analytic and taxonomic pursuits are engaged in solely for their own sakes, as if we should have been equally interested in classifying the one hundred and eighty-nine species of rhinogrades. On the contrary, it will be part of our purpose to argue that irony is a phenomenon of very considerable cultural and literary importance.

The question of the importance of irony is obviously not something that can be settled by determining to what extent it is or has been manifested in the various actions, utterances, thoughts, and products of all cultures and civilizations. If irony were largely confined to the Western world, as I have been led to believe (but I do not vouch for the fact), this would be of immense significance, but we should hardly think that irony was of less importance for not being universal. Nor is it relevant to the question of the importance of irony that more people lack a sense of irony than have one. The ordinary business of the world in which most of us are engaged most of the time could not be carried on in a spirit of irony. The importance of being ironical does not have to compete with the importance of being earnest or otherwise unironical. Indeed, should it ever seem to an ironist that the world's affairs really were being carried on ironically this would merely confirm the fact that they are not; if they were they could not seem to be. This is not a paradox but simply (or perhaps not simply) a way of saying that a sense of irony depends for its material upon a lack of a sense of irony in others, much as scepticism depends upon credulity.

It is of course another matter and a quite legitimate one to inquire what part is played in ordinary life by spoken irony, including the sub-forms of sarcasm, teasing, persiflage, under-statement, etc. And it would be very interesting to know the correlates of the absence, presence, and sophistication of these phenomena. But a systematic inquiry into the geographic (urban, provincial, or rustic), social, religious, educational, and occupa-tional background of 'colloquial' irony has yet to be made. And it would not be easy to make because 'ironically enough' the very presence of the inquirer would tend to destroy the rather intimate social *rapport* upon which these kinds of irony depend.

The simplest way to argue for the importance of irony in the literature of the Western world (leaving aside for the moment the wider question of its social and cultural importance) is to make a list of those writers of major status who are also ironists, an ironist being defined for this purpose as a writer whose work, or a substantial portion of whose work, is informed by a sense of irony. We cannot deny that irony is important if it is significantly present in the work of Aeschylus, Sophocles, Euripides, Aristophanes, Thucydides, Plato, Cicero, Horace, Catullus, Tacitus, Chaucer, Ariosto, Shakespeare, Cervantes, Pascal, Molière, Racine, Swift, Voltaire, Gibbon, Goethe, Stendhal, Byron, Heine, Kierkegaard,

Gogol, Dostoevsky, Flaubert, Renan, Ibsen, Tolstoy, Mark Twain, Henry James, Shaw, Chekhov, Pirandello, Proust, Thomas Mann, Kafka, and Brecht. Any undergraduate reading English and American literature could easily add a further twenty names without listing anyone born after 1900 or having recourse to such minor figures as Tourneur, Arbuthnot, Lamb, or Howells.

I do not think one could make a comparable list of great writers whose work is not ironical at all or is only occasionally, minimally, or doubtfully ironical. Certain great names come to mind, to be sure, in the fields of epic, lyric, and romance, but it is clear that we should have to supplement these with a far greater proportion of historians, philosophers, moralists, and orators, or admit imaginative writers of a lower rank. I shall not venture to propose a list of non-ironists, which would inevitably be found less acceptable than a list of ironists; but it might be worth remarking that an English list would draw most heavily upon nineteenth-century poetry.

THE IRONICAL AND THE NON-IRONICAL

The last two paragraphs, if we consider them for a moment, will suggest at least two lines of inquiry. First we can ask, and this in view of the fact that the non-literary arts are not very often ironical, whether there are grounds for thinking there is something in the very nature of literature which encourages ironic perception and expression, or whether there is something in the nature of the other arts which discourages irony; secondly, we can ask a similar question about drama and the theatre, since there is hardly a major dramatist who has failed to exploit the possibilities of dramatic irony. This second question may be postponed until we have become a little clearer about the nature of irony and its forms and functions. The first question, however, may be of some help here;

finding out why literature is more likely to be ironical than music and painting may be a way of discovering something about irony itself.

It is difficult, though not impossible, for some arts to be ironical. There is, I suppose, hardly any ironical architecture or landscape gardening. One reason is not far to seek; to be ironical is to be ironical about something, and the non-representational arts do not even refer to anything. Their object is not to represent things, which would be to make appearances, but to make things, to construct 'reality' in the shape of designs in space, lines, colours, stone, gold, musical sounds. These designs must have our un-divided attention, if we are attending at all, since there is nothing else to attend to: that is to say, these designs are not meant to remind us of anything else. They are as unironical as mathematical theorems or scientific hypotheses.

With representational art and with literature come various possibilities of escaping 'from Single Vision and Newton's Sleep', and consequently possibilities of irony. These possibilities are not always exploited, nor need they be. They are not exploited where the artist or the writer is single-mindedly engaged in getting something right, whether he calls it a perfect aesthetic design, or the absolute expression of some idea or feeling, or the true record of his soul. If it is the first of these, then it is irrelevant whether the art is representational or not; the countryside that is being painted is only a pretext for the painting. If it is the second or third, and we should add to these any wholly 'inspired' composition, then the content not merely takes priority over the means of expressing it but actually overwhelms and swallows up the expression, leav-ing us in direct, immediate contact with what is being expressed. It is in such cases that, in Wilfred Owen's words, 'the Poetry is in the pity.' The words disappear; the thoughts and feelings remain and become *our* thoughts and feelings: we become totally absorbed, quite carried away; room, chair, book, body, time vanish, their place being taken by pure experience. This is the literature of adventure and wish-fulfilment, of romantic, visionary, and prophetic writings, but it is also poetry at its most impassioned and 'musical'. And we are as far from irony when we are thus caught up in experience as we were when our undivided attention was given to a pure design.

We are now in a position to characterize some kinds of non-ironical art and literature as being indeed the object of 'single vision', immediately apprehensible because the formal properties either constitute an opaque surface, so to speak, which retains all our attention, or disappear in favour of the equally absorbing content they transparently reveal. Ironical art and literature should therefore, if we may go by contraries, have both surface and depth, both opacity and transparency, should hold our attention at the formal level while directing it to the level of content. Irony would combine MacLeish's Imagist or post-Imagist slogan:

> A poem should not mean
> But be

with Browning's 'messagism' (if we can apply the following lines to the little 'world' of a poem):

> This world's no blot for us,
> Nor blank; it means intensely, . . .

and rewrite them as

> An ironic poem should both mean
> And be

with the rider that the elements of 'meaning' and 'being' should oppose one another.

Is this what we find when music or painting is ironical? And is it all we find? The scope for irony in music seems not to be very large (if we exclude music that is accompanied by words): one piece of music can 'comment' ironically upon another or upon some other musical style or convention and this by way of parodic exaggeration or distortion or by incongruous juxtaposition or 'quoting'. In Tchaikovsky's *1812 Overture* there is a deliberate caricaturing of a few bars of *The Marseillaise* which directs us to adopt a certain attitude towards the Napoleonic *gloire*. But in doing so the music does not efface itself; it remains to confront what it refers to, there is both a surface and a depth. Whether this sort of thing could conceivably be the organizing principle of a musical composition and, if so, whether such a composition could be of equal dignity with non-parodic music will not be new questions to those who have found them answered in the affirmative, though of course only speculatively, in Thomas Mann's *Doctor Faustus*, the fictional biography of a musical composer. Vladimir Jankélévitch in *L'Ironie* (Paris, 1950) refers frequently to examples of ironical music.

In the graphic arts the possibilities for irony are very much greater. Like music and all other non-representational arts (despite what we said of architecture and gardening), painting can 'comment' ironically upon other works or upon a style or convention; but because it can be explicitly representational painting can also depict ironic situations. For example, a painting in which a respectably-dressed man is presented in an attitude of religious devotion is interpreted as a depiction of Tartuffe by a single incongruous detail – a lady's garter so placed as to suggest that it has been overlooked or imperfectly concealed.

What makes music and the graphic arts *less likely* than literature to be ironical is their greater reliance, implicit in the very nature of sound, colour, and line, upon a sensuous, attention-holding surface, though on this point a political cartoon might be found changing sides with a Tennysonian lyric. What makes it *possible* for them to be ironical is that they are in a sense 'languages'. The 'language' of an art, in this sense, is the set of accepted signs or conventions that has developed within the continuous tradition of each particular art. A few bars of *The Marseillaise* signifies 'France, in or after the Revolution'; played off-key the same bars suggest that one takes a critical attitude towards France (the date '1812' in the title gives us a more specific direction). The posture of Tartuffe signifies 'religious devotion'; the garter signifies 'illicit love'. All this explains why one cannot paint ironically an Alpine scene but only, say, a romantic Alpine scene, that is, an Alpine scene as regarded by others in a certain way. When, in the twentieth century, we look at one of Caspar David Friedrich's romantic landscapes we can easily recognize certain qualities that have become signs of Romanticism or even signs of this particular painter. It is these signs that an ironical painter will work with – and perhaps be abused by some backward art critic for being 'literary'.

In literature the scope for irony is wider still. Like all the arts, literature can parody the style of another artist or epoch. Like the graphic arts, it can depict ironic situations. But the language it employs is obviously far more able to deal with what people say, think, feel, and believe, and consequently with the differences between what people say and what they think and between what is believed to be and what is the case. And this precisely is the area within which irony operates. We have seen something of what a painter can do with a Tartuffe. He cannot do what Burns does in 'Holy Willie's Prayer':

> O L—d – yestreen – thou kens – wi' Meg —
> Thy pardon I sincerely beg!
> O may't ne'er be a living plague,
>   To my dishonor!
> And I'll ne'er lift a lawless leg
>   Again upon her. —
>
> Besides, I farther maun avow,
> Wi' Leezie's lass, three times – I trow —

But L—d, that friday I was fou
　When I cam near her;
Or else, thou kens, thy servant true
　Wad never steer her. —

Maybe thou lets this fleshly thorn
Buffet thy servant e'en and morn,
Lest he o'er proud and high should turn,
　That he's sae gifted;
If sae, thy hand maun e'en be borne
　Untill thou lift it. —

GETTING TO GRIPS WITH IRONY

Should anyone ever discover in himself the need to reduce another to mental and syntactic confusion, few things will be found so efficacious as asking him to write down on the spot a definition of irony. Admittedly, it sometimes happens that the person asked recalls some such definition as 'Irony is saying one thing but meaning the opposite'; but in this case one asks him if he would not regard as ironic the spectacle of a professional pickpocket having his own pocket picked while quietly going about his ordinary business, and, if so, how he thinks his definition ought to be adjusted to accommodate such instances as these. This generally restores the *status quo*.

The principal obstacle in the way of a simple definition of irony is the fact that irony is not a simple phenomenon. There is evidently a wide gap between the situational irony of which the single-minded pickpocket is a victim and the verbal irony, the academic subacidity of tone, with which I have been at pains to colour the preceding paragraph. And neither of these is obviously the same sort of thing as Orwell's *Animal Farm*, or Chaucer's self-presentation in *The Canterbury Tales*, or Thomas Mann's presentation of Hans Castorp in *The Magic Mountain*, or the fact that life moves irreversibly towards certain extinction, on the cosmic as on the individual scale, or Melville's *Billy Budd* in which peculiar circumstances inescapably oblige a naval commander to hang a man who he knows is entirely innocent, or the words with which a British statesman of the early nineteenth century (the story is R. H. Tawney's) is said to have crushed a clerical reformer, 'Things have come to a pretty pass if religion is going to interfere with private life', or one of the following passages:

'We been expecting you a couple of days and more. What's kep' you? – boat get aground?'
'Yes'm – [but] it warn't the grounding – that didn't keep us back but a little. We blowed out a cylinder-head.'
'Good gracious! anybody hurt?'
'No'm. Killed a nigger.'
'Well, it's lucky; because sometimes people do get hurt.'
  (Mark Twain, *Adventures of Huckleberry Finn*, Chapter XXXII)

To be plain, my good lord, it's but labour misplaced,
To send such good verses to one of your taste;
You've got an odd something – a kind of discerning,
A relish, a taste – sickened over by learning;
At least, it's your temper, as very well known,
That you think very slightly of all that's your own:
So perhaps, in your habits of thinking amiss,
You may make a mistake, and think slightly of this.
  (Goldsmith, 'The Haunch of Venison')

CONRADE: Away! You are an ass, you are an ass.
DOGBERRY: Dost thou not suspect my place? dost thou not suspect my years? O that he were here to write me down an ass! But, masters, remember that I am an ass; though it be not written down, yet forget not that I am an ass.
  (*Much Ado About Nothing*, IV, ii)

Nor do any of these instances of irony obviously resemble each other. Nor have I given examples representative of the whole range of irony.

A moment's reflection reveals, however, that the collection of ironies presented above is not entirely heterogeneous. In some of the instances there are people who appear to us or are presented to us as confident that everything is as they think it is, and we see them as being quite wrong. In other instances something is being said but something quite different is being conveyed. And the element common to these two groups is a contrast of an appearance and a reality. So it begins to look as if it might be possible to devise a definition that would cover the whole range of irony – provided we could first get agreement on what the whole range is. One or two of the instances cited above, for example, would not be accepted by everyone as being ironic.

In other words, irony not only takes very different forms but also, conceptually speaking, is still developing. In the sixteenth century 'irony' denoted only a figure of speech – which is not to say that what *we* call irony was not then practised or responded to but only that it was unnamed. Today 'irony' will mean different things to different people. Without concerning ourselves with the fact that this is no less true of different countries than of different people, we find in English-speaking countries on the one hand a tendency to stretch the concept of irony to the point of making it the essential or distinguishing quality of imaginative literature and on the other hand a tendency to restrict the concept to this or that form of 'pure' irony. So we have Cleanth Brooks arguing as if he thought that the modification of meaning that one element in a literary work necessarily undergoes as a result of the pressure of its context might be called irony ('Irony and "Ironic" Poetry', in *College English*, IX, 5 [1948], pp. 231–237). And we have A. H. Wright arguing that *Jonathan Wild* 'is not an ironic work, despite the author's free use of rhetorical irony', because 'Fielding's commitment is wholly to the values of Heartfree' ('Irony and Fiction', *Journal of Aesthetics and Art Criticism*, XII [1953], p. 116), and A. R. Thompson arguing in one place that irony is irony only when the effect is one of mingled pain and amusement and in another that, of the great tragic poets, Aeschylus, Sophocles, Euripides, Shakespeare, Corneille, Racine, and Ibsen, only Euripides and Ibsen were ironists since only these had a 'fundamentally ironical view of the world' (*The Dry Mock*, Berkeley, 1948, pp. 15 and 135 f.).

Still more unhelpful are those who refuse to define irony on the grounds that it is far too complex ever to disentangle (they don't say how far they got before they discovered this), while letting it be known that it is not so complex as entirely to escape them at the level of appreciation: 'We feel our way delicately and sensitively [one of them says, his feelers evidently in better shape than his mind] among many puzzling nuances of mood and tone.' But of all those who make it difficult to be clear about irony the worst are those who, being themselves both vague about irony and afraid of being thought too simple-minded to detect its presence, exploit the same qualities in their readers by making such prudently unspecific remarks as 'the obvious ironies of this passage. . .' But if one is not prepared to call the bluff of these ironiphiles the word 'irony' will retreat further into the conceptual fog that already half obscures it.

To add to our difficulties, people speak of irony as if it were indifferently something that goes on in the world: 'An ironic thing happened to me on the way to the theatre' – something that is characteristic of certain people: 'Euripides has a fundamentally ironic view of the world' – or something that is overtly behavioural: 'How have I deserved [said Mrs Slipslop] that my passion should be resulted and treated with ironing?' Moreover, one may think of irony primarily in terms of form or quality, of the ironist or the victim or the ironic observer, of the technique or the function or the effect. As a result a heterogeneous collection of names for 'kinds' of irony has come into existence; but far from adding up to a classification of irony it has merely increased the fogginess surrounding the word. For example, 'comic irony' is irony with a comic effect, but 'tragic irony' is the irony characteristic of tragedy; as such it is synonymous with 'Sophoclean irony', which is not confined to Sophocles' tragedies, and with 'dramatic irony', which is not confined to tragedy or even to drama – or even to literature. 'Irony of fate' is bound to be loosely used except by those who believe in fate and so are confused anyway. 'Self-irony' may mean being consciously ironical at one's own expense but it has been used for the irony of unconscious self-exposure. 'Irony of manner', in A. R. Thompson's *Dry Mock* (pp. 7–8), is presented as being synonymous with 'irony of character' and is illustrated by what I should regard as three different kinds of irony: the irony of unconscious self-exposure ('a windbag who is really a fool'), the irony of a Socrates deliberately presenting himself as a simpleton, and the irony in Saki's presentation of a child as both a murderer and, in the eyes of others, an innocent ten-year-old. Some kinds of irony have as yet no recognized name, and among those that have there is a good deal of duplication and overlapping.

2

The Nature of Irony

EARLY CONCEPTS OF IRONY

There are certain situations and utterances which we do not hesitate to call ironic. Odysseus returns to Ithaca and, sitting disguised as a beggar in his own palace, hears one of the suitors scouting the idea that he (Odysseus) could ever come home again. Later we read (Rieu's translation, but faithful to the sense of the original):

> Odysseus now had the bow in his hands and was twisting it about, testing it this way and that, for fear that the worms might have eaten into the horn in the long absence of its owner. The Suitors glanced at one another and gave vent to some typical comments: 'Ha! Quite the expert, with a critic's eye for bows! No doubt he collects them at home or wants to start a factory, judging by the way he twists it about, just as though he had learnt something useful in his life on the road!'

> (Book XXI, Penguin Classics)

We can scarcely doubt that the early audiences of the *Odyssey* responded to this situation in much the way we do, feeling that quite distinctive thrill at the spectacle of someone serenely unaware that the situation could be other than he thinks it is, while all the time it is the opposite of what he assumes. As for the sarcastic mockery, that too must strike us as having had, nearly three thousand years ago, essentially the same sort of effect as it has today.

I have chosen these two very early examples, one of Situational, one of Verbal Irony, not to suggest that irony was a Greek invention – I could have cited examples from Exodus and *Beowulf* – but in order first to indicate the antiquity of the phenomenon and then to make the point that irony, both as something we see and respond to and as something we practise, has to be distinguished both from the word 'irony' and the concept of irony. For the phenomenon existed before it was named and consequently before there could have been a concept of it; and the word existed before it was applied to the phenomenon. If Homer had a word for the suitors' mockery it was neither 'sarkasmos' nor 'eironeia'; the former did not acquire its modern meaning until very late and the latter did not mean Verbal Irony until the time of Aristotle. As for Situational Irony, the irony of the suitor's saying in Odysseus' presence that Odysseus would never come home, though it has been the staple irony of drama from Aeschylus to the present day, no one called it irony until, at the earliest, the late eighteenth century. And it does not appear that it was called anything else, though it is inconceivable that Sophocles or Shakespeare did not clearly recognize the dramatic effect of this kind of irony and certain that Racine did. The word 'irony' appears in some translations of the *Poetics* as a rendering of Aristotle's 'peripeteia' (sudden reversal of circumstances) which perhaps did duty for something of the meaning of dramatic irony.

'Eironeia' is first recorded in Plato's *Republic*. Applied to Socrates by one of his victims, it seems to have meant something like 'a smooth, low-down way of taking people in'. For Demosthenes an 'eiron' was one who evaded his responsibilities as a citizen by pretending unfitness. For Theophrastus an 'eiron' was evasive and non-committal, concealing his enmities, pretending friendship, misrepresenting his acts, never giving a straight answer. Miss Fairfax in *Emma* is a Theophrastian 'eiron' in refusing to express her own opinion: 'Was he handsome?' Emma asks, and can get no answer but 'I believe he was reckoned a very fine young man.' This may seem remote from any modern concept of irony. But the reader of Wayne Booth's *Rhetoric of Fiction* (Chicago, 1961) will see how the traditional ironic narrator, a Fielding or an Austen, has evolved, by way of the Flaubertian or Jamesian impersonal ironic narrator, into the narrator who has entirely abandoned any obligation to guide the judgement of his reader, and by so doing has become the modern counterpart of the old Greek 'eiron'.

Aristotle, however, possibly because he had Socrates in mind, had rated 'eironeia', in the sense of self-depreciative dissimulation, rather higher than its opposite, 'alazoneia' or boastful dissimulation; modesty, though only pretended, at least seems better bred than ostentation. At about the same time the word which at first denoted a mode of behaviour came also to be applied to a deceptive use of language; 'eironeia' is now a figure in rhetoric: to blame by ironical praise or to praise by ironical blame.

For Cicero, 'ironia' does not have the abusive meanings of the Greek word. In his usage it is either the rhetorical figure or the wholly admirable 'urbane pretence' of a Socrates, irony as a pervasive habit of discourse. So that when we use the word 'irony' of Socrates' way of pretending that he has high hopes of learning from his interlocutor what holiness or justice is, our concept of irony is a Roman one and not a Greek one, though it would be impossible to suppose that Plato was not as appreciative of the quality and effect of his irony as Cicero was. To these two meanings of irony recognized by Cicero, the rhetorician Quintilian added an intermediary one, irony as the elaboration of a figure of speech into an entire argument, the elaboration of some such irony as 'That was very intelligent of you!' into Erasmus's *In Praise of Folly*.

The word 'irony' does not appear in English until 1502 and did not come into general use until the early eighteenth century; Dryden, for example, used it only once. English, however, was rich in colloquial terms for verbal usages which we might regard as embryonic irony: fleer, flout, gibe, jeer, mock, scoff, scorn, taunt. Puttenham's *Arte of English Poesie* (ed. G. D. Willcock and A. Walker, London, 1936) actually translates 'ironia' as 'Drie Mock' and this clearly indicates an appreciation of the deadpan quality of a more subtle degree of verbal irony. The later seventeenth century and the eighteenth century made wide use of the words 'rally', 'banter', 'smoke', 'roast', and 'quiz' (1796), and these no doubt helped to keep the word 'irony' a literary word. Even now after three hundred and seventy years 'ironize' has still to be accepted; it is marked 'Obsolete' in the *O.E.D.*, does not appear in the *S.O.E.D.*, and is found only in the latest edition of *Webster's New International Dictionary*.

In England, as in the rest of modern Europe, the concept of irony developed very slowly. The more interesting meanings in Cicero and Quintilian, irony as a way of treating one's opponent in an argument and as the verbal strategy of a whole argument, were ignored at first, and for two hundred years and more irony was regarded principally as a figure of speech. The word was defined as 'saying the contrary of what one means', as 'saying one thing but meaning another', as 'praising in order to blame and blaming in order to praise', and as 'mocking and scoffing'. It was also used to mean dissimulation, even non-ironical dissimulation, understatement, and parody (once at least, by Pope). It was not until the first half of the eighteenth century, the age of *The Bickerstaff Papers*, *The History of John Bull*, *The Shortest Way with Dissenters*, *The Beggar's Opera*, *Jonathan Wild*, and *The Narrative of Dr Robert Norris*, concerning the Strange and Deplorable Frenzy of Mr John Dennis, an Officer of the Custom-House, that the meaning of the word 'irony' was again extended to include such works as these. A few writers, some with Cicero's discussion of Socrates clearly in their mind, are aware of irony as a mode of behaviour. Shaftesbury is noteworthy for having advised himself to adopt a 'soft irony', an ironic manner outwardly accommodating and amiable (though not devoid of raillery), inwardly serene and reserved.

By the middle of the eighteenth century the concept of irony in England, and, as far as I know, in other European countries, had scarcely evolved, in its broad outlines, beyond the point already reached in Quintilian. It is true that there are occasional passages, for example in Nashe (1589) and Burton (1621), which suggest that Situational or Dramatic Irony had been recognized as a form of irony, but these were isolated passages and had no effect at all upon the semantic development of the word. The concept of Dramatic Irony was not effectively introduced until the nineteenth century. It is also true that in 1748 Fielding used the word 'irony' with reference to the satiric strategy he practised of inventing a foolish character who would ineptly support and so unconsciously condemn views Fielding wished to condemn. But this kind of irony, as old in practice as the Socratic dialogues and Lucian's *Sale of Lives* and familiar as it is to every playgoer and novel-reader, has yet to be given a generally accepted name. In 1752 Richard Cambridge, the author of *The Scribleriad,* used the word 'irony' in connection with a contradictory outcome of events to the discomfiture of his foolish hero. But it is not certain that Cambridge saw this irony as an Irony of Events; he might well have thought of it as Verbal Irony: the promises of success made to Scriblerus were made ironically.

This outline history of the concept of irony to the middle of the eighteenth century has been based upon G. G. Sedgewick's *Of Irony, Especially in Drama* (Toronto, 1948) and Norman Knox's *The Word IRONY and Its Context, 1500–1755* (Durham, N.C., 1961), to which the reader is referred.

LATER CONCEPTS OF IRONY

It is in Germany at the very end of the eighteenth and the beginning of the nineteenth century that the word 'irony' takes on a number of new meanings. Some of these new meanings might well have developed in other countries; in fact no one has yet done the research that would conclusively establish historical priorities. The more important of the new meanings, however, clearly arose in the ferment of philosophical and aesthetic speculation that made Germany for many years the intellectual leader of Europe. The principal 'ironologists' of this period are Friedrich Schlegel, his brother August Wilhelm, and Karl Solger.

Neglecting strict chronology, I shall mention first the simpler of the new meanings. Both the Schlegels seem to be aware of the Irony of Events: speaking of *Troilus and Cressida* Friedrich Schlegel says, 'Long conversations are held, full of heroic sentiments, finely expressed, yet all apparently lead to nothing.' He also says there is 'tragische Ironie' in *King Lear* but does not elaborate. A. W. Schlegel sees as ironical Shakespeare's presentation of the

facility of self-deception, the half self-conscious hypocrisy towards ourselves, with which even noble minds attempt to disguise the almost inevitable influence of selfish motives in human nature.

(*Lectures on Dramatic Art and Literature* [1808],
trans. John Black, London, 1861, p. 369)

This is close to what I call the Irony of Self-betrayal (see Chapter 3, pp. 58–61).

More interesting is A. W. Schlegel's concept of irony as a balancing of serious and comic or fanciful and prosaic:

Irony . . . is a sort of confession interwoven into the representation itself, and more or less distinctly expressed, of its overcharged one-sidedness in matters of fancy and feeling, and by means of which the equipoise is again restored.

(Ibid., p. 227)

This he finds both in Gozzi's fairy-tale dramas with their contrasting masked scenes and in Shakespeare, where the comic sub-plot sometimes 'comments' on or parodies the main plot. This kind of irony was rediscovered by I. A. Richards who defines irony, in a similar way, as 'the bringing in of the opposite, the complementary impulses' in order to achieve a 'balanced poise'. (*Principles of Literary Criticism*, 2nd ed., London, 1926, p. 250). This was to become the basis of the 'New Critics' ' concept of irony.

A. W. Schlegel was unable, however, to relate the ironic and the tragic: 'No doubt, wherever the proper tragic enters everything like irony immediately ceases; . . . [as also] where the subjection of mortal beings to an inevitable destiny demands the highest degree of seriousness' (Ibid., p. 370). Karl Solger, on the other hand, claims that genuine irony 'begins with the contemplation of the world's fate in the large' (quoted from René Wellek, *A History of Modern Criticism: The Romantic Age*, London, 1955, p. 300). And before him, Friedrich Schlegel had come to believe that irony was the 'recognition of the fact that the world in its essence is paradoxical and that an ambivalent attitude alone can grasp its contradictory totality' (Wellek, p. 14). The idea of there being an irony in the fundamental incongruities of man and the rest of the universe, of life and death, of the spiritual and the material, was, under the names of World Irony, Cosmic Irony, or Philosophical Irony, to play an increasing part in the history of the concept of irony (see Chapter 4, pp. 66–77). At a lower level, G. H. Schubert, writing in 1821, saw as irony any naturally occurring incongruity such as, for example, the juxtapositions in the natural scale of rational man and absurd ape, noble horse and ridiculous ass.

Both the Schlegels and, following them, Karl Solger and others used the term 'irony' in speaking of the objectivity, 'indifference', and freedom of the artist in relation to his work. Most novelists and dramatists, A. W. Schlegel says, embody their own subjectivity in one character or one viewpoint with which the reader too is supposed to be in sympathy. But Shakespeare, though he

endows each of his characters with so much life that we cannot
doubt his sympathy for them, is equally detached from them all;
so that his plays do not express his own subjectivity but 'express
the whole world' and this, Goethe says, is the mark of a real
artist. This irony of the aloof godlike author which the Schlegels
found in Aristophanes, Petrarch, Cervantes, Shakespeare, Goethe,
and others was also, in both theory and practice, the irony of
Flaubert, Joyce, and Thomas Mann.

If, now, we complicate this, as Friedrich Schlegel did, by
pointing out that there are ironies inherent in the very fact of
being an artist, we shall have yet another concept of irony – that
of Romantic Irony – the irony of the fully-conscious artist whose
art is the ironical presentation of the ironic position of the fully-
conscious artist. The artist is in an ironic position for several
reasons: in order to write well he must be both creative and
critical, subjective and objective, enthusiastic and realistic,
emotional and rational, unconsciously inspired and a conscious
artist; his work purports to be about the world and yet is fiction;
he feels an obligation to give a true or complete account of reality
but he knows this is impossible, reality being incomprehensibly
vast, full of contradictions, and in a continual state of becoming,
so that even a true account would be immediately falsified as soon
as it was completed. The only possibility open for a real artist is to
stand apart from his work and at the same time incorporate this
awareness of his ironic position into the work itself and so create
something which will, if a novel, not simply be a story but rather
the telling of a story complete with the author and the narrating,
the reader and the reading, the style and the choosing of the style,
the fiction and its distance from fact, so that we shall regard it as
being ambivalently both art and life. The concept of Romantic
Irony is not an easy one and it has been widely misunderstood and
misrepresented, particularly by American literary critics. The best
way to come to an understanding of it and an appreciation of its

importance in modern self-conscious literature is to read Thomas Mann's novels, especially *Joseph and His Brothers* and *Doctor Faustus*.

The next name in the history of the concept of irony is that of Connop Thirlwall who in 1833 published a long article 'On the Irony of Sophocles'. Thirlwall had studied German philosophy and literature, and his article owes something to German concepts of irony, but he had ideas of his own. Besides Verbal or Rhetorical Irony he distinguishes 'Dialectical Irony' (the ironic strategy of a Socrates), which is only a new name for a kind of irony already recognized by Cicero, and 'Practical Irony' which, as its name implies, is 'independent of all forms of speech' and may be found in life as well as in literature. He gives a number of instances of Practical Irony, several of which have since acquired more specific names. (This article may be found in *The Philological Museum*, Vol. II).

Timon in *Timon of Athens* is ironical in giving gold to the thieves since this apparent kindness is really intended to do them harm. The contradictory outcome of events is ironical whether fortunate or unfortunate and whether the victim is an individual or a whole civilization; Thirlwall here seems to conceive of an irony without any ironist, which is a highly significant development. In speaking of Sophocles, however, and the Irony of Fate, there is a suggestion of fate as a semi-personified force: 'the contrast between man with his hopes, fears, wishes, and undertakings, and a dark, inflexible fate, affords abundant room for the exhibition of tragic irony' (p. 493).

Even more significant is the suggestion that irony may reside in the attitude of an ironic observer or, rather, in the situation observed:

There is always a slight cast of irony in the grave, calm, respectful attention impartially bestowed by an intelligent judge on two contending parties, who are pleading their causes before him with all the earnestness of deep conviction, and of excited feeling. What makes the contrast interesting is, that the right and the truth lie on neither side exclusively . . . here the irony lies not in the demeanour of the judge, but is deeply seated in the case itself, which seems to favour each of the litigants, but really eludes them both.

(pp. 489 – 90)

On p. 525 Thirlwall cites the *Antigone* of Sophocles as ironical in that it impartially presents two equal and opposite points of view. The germ of this concept of irony is already in Friedrich Schlegel's 'Irony is a form of paradox' but Thirlwall even if he had read this in Schlegel is much more explicit. The later history of the concept of irony elevates this kind of irony to a central position: in any paradox there are two contradictory truths; an ambiguity is ironical if the two co-existent meanings are opposed: in a dilemma there are two equally impossible courses of action, both perhaps obligatory as in those heroic dramas in which the hero must sin against either Duty or Love. This may be raised to a philosophical level:

[Irony is] a view of life which recognizes that experience is open to multiple interpretations, of which no *one* is simply right, and that the co-existence of incongruities is a part of the structure of existence.

(Samuel Hynes, *The Pattern of Hardy's Poetry*, Chapel Hill, N.C., 1961, pp. 41 – 42)

Another passage from Thirlwall reveals the influence of the German theorists:

The dramatic poet is the creator of a little world, in which he rules with absolute sway, and may shape the destinies of the imaginary beings to whom he gives life and breath according to any plan that he may choose. . . . From this [mimic] sphere [of his creating] . . . he himself stands aloof. The eye with which he views his microcosm, and the creatures who move in it, will not be one of human friendship, nor of brotherly kindness, nor of parental love: it will be that with which he imagines that the invisible power who orders the destiny of man might regard the world and its doings.

(pp. 490 – 1)

This idea of a play and Thirlwall's concept of the Irony of Fate both involve the notion of the victim of irony as ignorant of what is already predestined. Putting them together, Thirlwall arrives at the concept of Dramatic Irony, or 'tragic irony' as he calls it, the irony of a Clytemnestra saying, having heard a false report of the death of Orestes who has secretly come home to kill her:

> Now I am free,
> Free of all fear of him, . . .
> And I can live in peace.

This concept of irony is now perfectly familiar in English-speaking countries, but much less so on the Continent.

The reader who has been looking forward to an equally leisurely progress through the period that follows Thirlwall's article must now have it broken to him that, strange as it may seem, this article was the last *major* step in the long history of the concept of irony. All the principal kinds of irony that have been practised and all the classes of phenomena that we now regard as ironic have been, more or less clearly, recognized as irony. Nearly everything since can be classed *either* as restatements, rediscoveries, distinctions between 'real' and 'so-called' irony, clarifications, classifications or sub-classifications, *or* as more general discussions of the nature of irony, its place in man's intellectual and spiritual life, its place in relation to other literary modes.

Kierkegaard's thinking on irony, from his 1841 thesis, *The Concept of Irony*, onwards, is directed very largely towards a placing of irony between what he calls the aesthetic and the ethical 'stages' of spiritual development. For Kierkegaard 'whoever has essential irony has it all day long'; he is not ironical from time to time or in this or that direction but considers the totality of existence *sub specie ironiae* and is never ironical in order to be admired as an ironist. For Amiel, irony is Philosophical Irony, he has a concept of a law of irony: 'Absurdity is interwoven with life: real beings are animated contradictions, absurdities brought into action' (*Journal Intime*, 15 November 1876). For Heine, Baudelaire, Nietzsche, and Thomas Mann irony is principally Romantic Irony, but Heine is aware of the self-protective function of irony and of irony as a presentation of such fundamental opposites as soul and body.

In the first half of this century the word 'irony' was again used (see A. W. Schlegel on Gozzi above) of literature which, for various reasons, juxtaposes, without comment, opposite or merely different points of view. The object of this ironic procedure might be to achieve a balanced all-round view, to express one's awareness of the complexity of life or the relativity of values, to express a larger and richer meaning than would be possible with direct statement, to avoid being over-simple or over-dogmatic, to show that one has earned the right to an opinion by showing that one is aware of its potentially destructive opposite. In the discussions of this kind of irony there is much that calls to mind the phenomenon of protective colouring familiar to the entomologist. In order to survive in an environment of predatory critics, literature has to disguise itself either as criticism or as something even the most rapacious critic would do well to be extremely wary of.

THE ELEMENTS OF IRONY

Any attempt to define the nature of irony faces a number of difficulties. In Chapter 1, attention was drawn to the diversity of forms that irony may take, to the different points of view from which irony may be approached, and to the fact that the concept of irony is still evolving.

Something more might be said about the last of these. In principle, of course, irony is whatever we agree to call irony. In practice, however, we do not all agree on all points; what we achieve is at best an uneasy, unstable compromise between the tendency to restrict the application of the word to what people have, in the immediate past, agreed to call irony (in so far as they *have* agreed), the tendency to apply a qualitative criterion (for example, Thompson's criterion of a painful *and* comic effect – see pp. 33–35 below), and the tendency to apply the word to anything which resembles irony in form, function, or effect, or which regularly accompanies irony, or which has only *some* of the properties of irony as hitherto recognized. The concept of irony at any time may be likened to a ship at anchor when wind, tide, and current are each strong enough to be dragging it slowly from its anchorage. An account of irony ought therefore to indicate not only the agreed or 'central' properties of irony but also the various directions in which the concept of irony shows a tendency to drift.

It is not particularly difficult to define Verbal Irony in a reasonably satisfactory and memorable form. It is not particularly easy to define Situational Irony or even its sub-form Dramatic Irony, and this, incidentally, might in part explain the long delay in conceptualizing it. To define irony in such a way as to do justice to both the principal kinds (Verbal Irony and Situational Irony) is desperately difficult. What *can* be done is to isolate the various elements, properties, or features that have been put forward as basic to all forms of irony. Phenomena which have only some of these features or have them all but some in only a weakened form will generally be regarded as not irony at all or only as quasi-irony; but they may indicate the directions in which the concept of irony may develop.

The element of 'innocence' or 'confident unawareness'

We can begin with the classical notions of simulation and dissimulation: pretending to be what one is not and pretending not to be what one is. Allan Rodway, in an article 'Terms for Comedy' (*Renaissance and Modern Studies*, VI, 1962, p. 113), writes:

So many critics today, especially in America, find irony under every stone that a reminder of its original meaning may not come amiss – *eirôneia,* 'assumed ignorance', from *eirôn,* 'a dissembler'. The sense of a dissembling that is meant to be seen through must remain fundamental if the word is to have any consistent function.

Eleanor Hutchens too speaks (*Irony in* TOM JONES, Alabama, 1965, p. 20) of the 'basic concept of a purposeful deception'.

So Socrates, Chaucer, Pascal (in his *Provincial Letters*), and Matthew Arnold (in *Friendship's Garland*) pretend to be naïve, credulous, simple-minded, ingenuously indignant, blindly enthusiastic, complacently or confidently foolish. So Swift, in *An Argument to Prove that the Abolishing of Christianity may . . . be Attended with Some Inconveniences,* pretended to be defending false Christianity; and in this epigram

> A Petty Sneaking Knave I knew —
> O Mr. Cromek, how do ye do?

Blake pretends that Mr Cromek's sudden appearance has stopped him from revealing the name of the sneaking knave. There is, in fact, no difficulty in finding examples of irony that exhibit some kind of deception or pretence. But all deceptions are not ironical, and some irony perhaps does not involve pretence or dissembling.

Rodway's answer to the first objection is that ironical dissembling is distinguished from non-ironical dissembling in that it 'is meant to be seen through'. This seems to be a satisfactory answer provided we understand that irony is not necessarily meant to be seen through by the victim of one's irony but only by the audience. Sometimes, perhaps, the sole audience is the ironist himself.

As to the second objection, it is ironic that the action Oedipus takes to avoid his fate serves only to bring it about. It is ironic that he lays a curse upon the unknown killer of King Laius, only to discover that he has cursed himself. We would call ironic the spectacle of a pickpocket having his own pocket picked while absorbed in picking others' pockets. We would call 'ironic' this French street-name, 'Impasse de l'Enfant Jésus'. But there seems in none of these to be any element of pretence or deception. If one believed, however, that some things that happen are the work of a personal but non-human agency, whether god or devil, or a personified Fate, Life, or Fortune, then clearly such an agency could be an ironical deceiver leading us up the garden path or concealing obvious contradictions from our sight.

Othello saw Situational Irony as a joke played upon men by the devil:

> O 'tis the spite of hell, the arch-fiend's mock
> To lip a wanton in a secure couch
> And to suppose her chaste.

When we are in a great hurry to go out and a shoelace breaks we are inclined to say, 'That's just the sort of thing that *would* happen', as if there were Things motivated by malice. Haakon Chevalier seems to think that the victim does not wholly get rid of the

suspicion that . . . there exists a deliberate mockery [at his expense]. This theoretical imputation of mockery is an atavistic survival of the old and enduring consciousness of the 'jealousy of the gods'.

(*The Ironic Temper*, New York, 1932, p. 42)

According to Hutchens (who asserts more than she has evidence for):

It is usual to imagine Fate (or whatever idea of causality we may hold) as a deliberate deceiver: . . . one assumes (if only figuratively) that there must be planning behind a process which first arouses expectation and then neatly reverses it.

(*Irony in* TOM JONES, p. 15)

The point at issue is whether one can see or feel some event or situation as ironic without also assuming the existence of a non-human mocker. To answer in the affirmative is in effect to agree to a classification of irony into two basic groups: one the irony of an ironist intentionally being ironical (this is ordinarily called Verbal Irony but, since an ironist can employ other media, it might more comprehensively be called Behavioural Irony); the other the irony of an ironic situation or event in which there is no ironist but always both a victim and an observer (this kind is ordinarily called Situational Irony but could be called Unintentional or Unconscious Irony). If we take this point of view, we can see the assumption of an ironical personified Fate as the bridge by which the concept of irony crossed over to take possession of the hitherto unnamed Situational Ironies.

If there can be irony without an ironist, there can be irony without any deceiver or pretender. This 'basic feature' need not be abandoned, however, though it may have to be modified. The solution depends upon seeing the victim of irony as something other than the victim of a mere deception, whether he is deceived by someone or by appearances. A man does not become a victim of irony by diving into an empty swimming-pool under the impression that it is full. Something more is needed than error, ignorance, imperceptiveness, or even imprudence. But if this man had been the diving-instructor himself, or if he had been told the pool was empty and had chosen to know better, we would regard his mistake as ironic. What has been added to the deception by appearances is an element of blind self-confidence or serene unawareness; the diving-instructor, of all men, should have been aware of the possibility of making this mistake. This blind self-confidence or something like it characterizes Oedipus, the pick-pocket, and the man who can consciously name a street 'Impasse de l'Enfant Jésus' and not be conscious of the shattering incongruity the name contains. The victim of irony does not need to be, though he often is, arrogantly, wilfully blind; he need only reveal by word or action that he does not even remotely suspect that things may not be what he ingenuously supposes them to be.

The basic element is a serene, confident unawareness coloured, in practice, by varying degrees of arrogance, conceitedness, complacency, naïvety, or innocence. Other things being equal, the greater the victim's blindness, the more striking the irony. It goes without saying that the ironic observer must be aware of the victim's unawareness as well as of the real situation.

The victim of irony then is not simply deceived by appearances, or even self-deceived, though this comes nearer to the idea of a serenely confident unawareness. Can we now return to the ironist and see his deception or pretence in similar terms? A practised ironist can convey his real meaning without showing the least consciousness of there being any meaning but the ostensible one. In this he resembles the victim of irony who unconsciously reveals what a fool he is in words which he thinks are impressively wise. The victim of irony is serenely unaware that his words or actions convey a quite different meaning or assumption; the ironist 'innocently' pretends to have this serene unawareness:

> In relation to a foolishly inflated wisdom which knows about everything it is ironically correct to go along with it, to be transported by all this knowledge, to goad it on. . . , although through all this the ironist is himself aware that the whole thing is empty and void of content. In relation to an insipid and inane enthusiasm it is ironically correct to outbid this with ever more and more elated exultation and praise, although the ironist is himself aware that this enthusiasm is the greatest foolishness in the world.
>
> (Kierkegaard, *The Concept of Irony*, trans. Lee M. Capel, London, 1966, p. 266)

Ironists such as Shakespeare, Fielding, Jane Austen, Mark Twain, and Evelyn Waugh endow fictitious characters with the same qualities as Socrates or Chaucer pretend to have – simple-mindedness or foolish complacency. At a lower level mockery often takes the form of mimicking the defects of the person being mocked.

A curious consequence of this is that doubts occasionally arise as to whether an utterance or a word is intentionally ironical or unconsciously ironic. And there may be a doubt as to where the irony of a work is located; the *Mona Lisa* has been interpreted both as a portrait of someone smiling ironically and as an ironical portrait of someone smiling with foolish self-satisfaction.

The contrast of reality and appearance

According to Haakon Chevalier, 'The basic feature of every Irony is a contrast between a reality and an appearance' (*The Ironic Temper*, p. 42). An ironist seems to be saying one thing but is really saying something quite different; a victim of irony is confident that things are what they seem and unaware that they are really quite different. We can rephrase this so as to make the element of 'confident unawareness' more explicit: the ironist presents an appearance and pretends to be unaware of a reality while the victim is deceived by an appearance and is unaware of a reality.

It is when we lend 'reality' and 'appearance' absolute value that Chevalier's statement becomes doubtful. When Swift says in the *Argument Against Abolishing Christianity*:

> It must be allowed indeed that to Break an *English* Free-born Officer only for Blasphemy, was, to speak the gentlest of such an Action, a very high strain of absolute Power,

his real meaning is that it was perfectly right and proper to cashier an officer for so heinous a crime. But a modern reader might be inclined to interpret this literally and so mistake appearance for reality. Similarly, changes in attitudes operate to reverse reality and appearance in Johnson's ironical *reductio ad absurdum* of Soame Jenyns' philosophical speculations:

> As we drown whelps and kittens, they [Jenyns' superior beings] amuse themselves, now and then, with sinking a ship, and stand round the fields of Blenheim, or the walls of Prague, as we encircle a cockpit.

As we shoot a bird flying, they take a man in the midst of his business or pleasure, and knock him down with an apoplexy. Some of them, perhaps, are virtuosi, and delight in the operations of an asthma, as a human philosopher in the effects of the air-pump. To swell a man with a tympany is as good sport as to blow a frog. Many a merry bout have these frolick beings at the vicissitudes of an ague, and good sport it is to see a man tumble with an epilepsy, and revive and tumble again, and all this he knows not why.

Nineteenth-century cosmic ironists would be inclined to think this a very probable explanation of the human condition. Hardy, for example, closes his *Tess of the D'Urbervilles* with these words: ' "Justice" was done, and the President of the Immortals, in Aeschylean phrase, had ended his sport with Tess.' We must conclude therefore that what is 'appearance' and what is 'reality' in irony are no more than what the ironist or ironic observer take them to be, from which it follows that irony itself is not invulnerable to further irony from a new vantage-ground.

The more familiar type of irony is that in which a 'reality' obviously corrects an 'appearance'. We have, however, in speaking of Thirlwall and elsewhere, found a type of irony which consists of a juxtaposition of equal and opposite propositions, situations, or values. A paradox, for example, juxtaposes two truths and does not correct a falsehood by a truth; Heine sees *Don Quixote* as an ironic allegory of the soul and the body, each of which is sometimes in the right and sometimes in the wrong; in the same class are all ironic dilemmas and other 'impossible situations'.

This type of irony may be seen as consisting, none the less, of a contrasting reality and appearance. Either the paradox or dilemma only *appears* to be such, or the victim gratuitously assumes that he lives in a world in which impossible situations ought to stay impossible, a world which is organized according to the principles of justice and logic, whereas the ironist or ironic observer sees the world as in reality absurd or contradictory. It has to be admitted, however, that most people see the irony as inherent in the paradox or dilemma and not in the contrast of a true and a false picture of reality. This is one way in which the concept of irony is drifting away from the 'central' feature of a contrasting appearance and reality.

The word 'contrast' in Chevalier's proposition is worth attending to. It would hardly be ironic if a man who seemed to be Swedish turned out to be really Norwegian – unless Sweden and Norway were at war. It is less ironical to call a girl beautiful if she is plain than if she is hideous. So we might conclude, first, that irony demands an opposition or incongruity of appearance and reality and, secondly, that, other things being equal, the greater the contrast the more striking the irony.

Recently, however, there has been a tendency to equate subtlety in irony with a lesser degree or even an absence of contrast, so that any ambiguity may be regarded as ironical. And since practically all literature says more than it seems to be saying, if only because it contains the universal in the particular, practically all literature can be called ironical. Some of the responsibility for this tendency must be borne by Cleanth Brooks. Needing a term with which to speak of the difference between the meaning of an element in a poem when regarded in isolation or as it appears in a paraphrase and the full force and meaning it has in its context, he pitched, with some misgivings but not enough, upon the word 'irony': 'Irony is the most general term that we have for the kind of qualification which the various elements in a context receive from the context' (*The Well-Wrought Urn*, London, 1949, p. 191). To accept this is to regard all discourse as ironical since in any discourse the context modifies its elements. But if we regard all discourse as ironical, what word do we use for distinguishing 'Holy Willie's Prayer' from the General Confession of the Anglican prayer-book? Anyone disposed to be fair to Cleanth Brooks can add that in practice he concerned himself with contrasts and not just differences in meaning, though the contrasts he discussed were unemphasized, unexploited, or merely potential.

The comic element

A. R. Thompson argues in his *Dry Mock* that the ironic contrast must, to be ironic, affect us as both painful and comic:

> In irony, emotions clash. . . . it is both emotional and intellectual – in its literary manifestations, at any rate. To perceive it one must be detached and cool; to feel it one must be pained for a person or ideal gone amiss. Laughter rises but is withered on the lips. Someone or something we cherish is cruelly made game of; we see the joke but are hurt by it.
>
> It follows from this view that contrasts which conform exactly to the objective definitions of irony are not ironical at all when they do not rouse these conflicting feelings.
>
> (p. 15)

There are several things one might want to say to this. And first of all, that we will still continue to call such passages as the following ironical even though they do not affect us as painful:

> But natheless, certeyn,
> I kan right now no thrifty tale seyn
> That Chaucer, thogh he kan but lewedly
> On metres and on rymyng craftily,
> Hath seyd hem in swich Englissh as he kan
> Of olde tyme, as knoweth many a man.
> (Chaucer, *Canterbury Tales,* Introduction to
> *The Man of Law's Tale*)

The history of [Arminius von Thunder-ten-Tronckh's] family has been written by the famous Voltaire in his *Candide*; but I doubt whether an honest man can in conscience send the British public to even the historical works of that dangerous author.

(Matthew Arnold, *Friendship's Garland*)

In fact, Thompson himself finds he cannot do without the word 'irony' for speaking about situations which his theory forbids him to call irony. In a discussion of Molière's *School for Wives*, in which 'the jealous guardian is confided in throughout by both lover and ward and yet cannot prevent their union,' he says, 'So far as irony is a matter of device to bring about results exactly the reverse of a character's intentions, this is masterly irony. But we, as spectators, are not involved emotionally except to be amused' (p. 100).

Secondly, we might want to argue that when we do find both amusement and hurt in irony they do not have the same sort of basis. The comic element seems to be inherent in the formal properties of irony: the basic contradiction or incongruity coupled with a real or a pretended confident unawareness. No man wittingly contradicts himself (unless with the intention of resolving the contradiction at another level, in which case there is no real contradiction); consequently, the appearance of an intentional contradiction sets up a psychic tension which can only find a resolution in laughter. On the other hand, the painful element Thompson postulates for irony does not arise from any formal property but only from the sympathy we may feel towards the victim. And this will vary according to the way the irony is presented to us. It is to be noticed that whereas Thompson can provide many examples of what, according to him, *would* be irony if only there were a painful element, he offers no examples of 'contrasts which conform exactly to the objective definitions of irony' but which cannot be called ironic because they have no comic element.

This is not a question which can very profitably be discussed in the abstract. We are not so constituted as always to react to the same event in the same way, or in the same way for any length of time. Moreover, the terms available as names for these fluctuating states of mind may be grossly inadequate. We can concede that in some ironies the comic element may be slight and the painful element large, and that, other things being equal, irony is more effective or more striking if it has a painful as well as a comic effect. And finally we might concede that we have to feel something of the force of the victim's point of view or of the ironist's pretended point of view but not necessarily that degree of sympathy which would generate feelings of pain. If we did not feel, if we did not believe in, Oedipus' confidence that he was not the guilty one, we should not feel the contrast of appearance and reality. Similarly with Verbal Irony: the pretended meaning must have some force or body to it and not be transparent to the point of non-existence.

The element of detachment

We have now presented, as basic features for all irony, (i) a contrast of appearance and reality, (ii) a confident unawareness (pretended in the ironist, real in the victim of irony) that the appearance is only an appearance, and (iii) the comic effect of this unawareness of a contrasting appearance and reality. There is yet another feature of irony which appears regularly in discussions of irony. We can choose from among a number of terms: detachment, distance, disengagement, freedom, serenity, objectivity, dispassion, 'lightness', 'play', urbanity. The quality these words seek to identify is a quality that seems sometimes to reside in the ironist's pretended manner and sometimes in the real attitude of the ironist or the ironic observer. For example, one of the great ironists of this century, Thomas Mann, wrote explicitly of the need for *Heiterkeit* (serenity) in the face of the unanswerable questions life confronts us with:

Oh . . . it is all too exciting and solemn for words! And just because it is so solemn it must be treated with a light touch. For lightness, my friend, flippancy, the artful jest, that is God's very best gift to man, the profoundest knowledge we have of that complex, questionable thing we call life. God gave it to humanity, that life's terribly serious face might be forced to wear a smile.

(Joseph in *Joseph the Provider*, VI,
translated by H. T. Lowe-Porter, London, 1956)

This lightness may be but is not necessarily an inability to feel the terrible seriousness of life; it may be a refusal to be overwhelmed by it, an assertion of the spiritual power of man over existence. Swift felt the lacerating effect of savage indignation but his irony plays it cool in even his bitterest work, his 'modest proposal' that the English Protestant landlords in Ireland should restore the country to economic health by buying and eating the babies of the destitute unemployed Catholics:

As to our City of *Dublin*, Shambles may be appointed for this purpose, in the most convenient parts of it, and Butchers we may be assured will not be wanting, although I rather recommend buying the Children alive, and dressing them hot from the Knife, as we do *roasting Pigs*.

A feeling that might most naturally have found expression in a howl of anguish and despair has here been transformed into a rationally argued economic treatise coloured only by the modest proposer's complacent, self-congratulatory tone. Swift has been able to control the impulse to blurt out what he feels: there has been a pause, a distancing, an intellectualizing, and, in the end, while nothing could have had a greater emotional impact, something has been made as well as said.

The concept of detachment seems to be implicit in the concept of pretence, since the ironist's ability to pretend attests a degree of control over more immediate responses. It seems also to be implicit in the concept of the ironic observer for whom an ironic situation or event is a spectacle, which is to say, something observed from the outside.

What an ironic observer typically feels in the presence of an ironic situation may be summed up in three words: superiority, freedom, amusement. Goethe says that irony raises a man 'above happiness or unhappiness, good or evil, death or life'. Amiel compares 'the feeling which makes men earnest [with] the irony which leaves them free', and Thomas Mann speaks of irony as

> an all-embracing crystal-clear and serene glance, which is the very glance of art itself, that is to say: a glance of the utmost freedom and calm and of an objectivity untroubled by any moralism.
>
> ('The Art of the Novel' in *The Creative Vision*, ed. Haskell M. Block and Herman Salinger, New York, 1960, p. 88)

In Lucretius, Lucan, Cicero, Dante, Chaucer, Shakespeare, Bacon, Heine, Nietzsche, Flaubert, Amiel, Tennyson, Meredith, not to mention the Bible, we can find the idea that looking down from on high upon the doings of men induces laughter or at least a smile.

The ironic observer's awareness of himself as observer tends to enhance his feeling of freedom and induce a mood perhaps of serenity, or joyfulness, or even exultation. His awareness of the victim's unawareness invites him to see the victim as bound or trapped where he feels free; committed where he feels disengaged; swayed by emotions, harassed, or miserable, where he is dispassionate, serene, or even moved to laughter; trustful, credulous, or naïve, where he is critical, sceptical, or content to suspend judgement. And where his own attitude is that of a man whose world appears real and meaningful, he will see the victim's world as illusory or absurd. Distinguishing the different kinds of heroes in fiction, Northrop Frye writes:

> If inferior in power or intelligence to ourselves, so that we have the sense of looking down on a scene of bondage, frustration, or absurdity, the hero belongs to the *ironic* mode.
>
> (*Anatomy of Criticism*, Princeton, N.J., 1957, p. 34)

From this point of view the pure or archetypal ironist is God — 'He that sitteth in the heavens shall laugh: the Lord shall have them in derision.' He is the ironist *par excellence* because he is omniscient, omnipotent, transcendent, absolute, infinite, and free. In Karl Solger's view:

> Supreme Irony reigns in the conduct of God as he creates men and the life of men. In earthly art Irony has this meaning – conduct similar to God's.
>
> (Quoted from Sedgewick, op. cit., p. 17)

The archetypal victim of irony is man, seen, *per contra,* as trapped and submerged in time and matter, blind, contingent, limited, and unfree – and confidently unaware that this is his predicament. 'We laugh', says Bergson, 'every time a person gives us the impression of being a thing.'

We have already seen in the references to Johnson and Hardy (pp. 30–31), that the gods can be conceived of as spectators of an ironic show they have themselves put on; in their cat-and-mouse game they have us in their power but pretend not to have in the hope that we will think we are free and attempt to behave accordingly. It is interesting to find that God was also thought of as a dramatist or novelist and, conversely, writers were thought of as gods, and this with reference to their power not only of creating an independent world but also of playing with its inhabitants. Several passages may be cited which lay some stress upon the detachment of the artist from his creation and the complementary blindness and helplessness of his creatures. Diderot's novel *Jacques le fataliste* (1773) begins with the doctrine of determinism presented in terms of authorship: 'Everthing that happens to us here on earth, good or bad, was written on high.' Thereafter the work plays variations on the determinism: freewill problem as it affects mankind, authors, characters, and readers. Friedrich Schlegel, writing of Goethe's *Wilhelm Meister* (1795), says:

> The author himself seems to take the characters and incidents so lightly and whimsically, scarcely ever mentioning his hero without

irony and smiling down upon his masterpiece itself from the height of his spirit.

('Über Goethes Meister', 1798, *Kritische Ausgabe*, II, ed. Hans Eichner, Paderborn, 1967, p. 133)

The concept is clearly presented by Thirlwall (see above, pp. 22–23 and in Heine's *Confessions* (1854):

Alas, the irony of God weighs heavily upon me. The great Author of the universe, the Aristophanes of heaven, wished to show me – the little, earthly, so-called German Aristophanes – as glaringly as possible what feeble little jests my most bitter sarcasms were in comparison with His own, and how inferior I was to Him in humour and in giant wit.

(*Confessions*, 1854, quoted from *The Poetry and Prose of Heinrich Heine*, ed. and trans. Frederick Ewen, New York, 1948, p. 489)

In 1852, in a letter to Louise Colet, Flaubert wrote:

Quand est-ce qu'on écrira les faits au point de vue d'une *blague supérieure*, c'est-à-dire comme le bon Dieu les voit, d'en haut?

(When will people begin to write down the facts as if it were all a divine joke, that is to say, as the Lord sees them, from above?)

And in 1857 in a letter to Madame de Chantepie:

L'artiste doit être dans son oeuvre comme Dieu dans la création, invisible et tout-puissant; qu'on le sente partout, mais qu'on ne le voie pas.

(The artist should be in his work as God is in the created world, invisible and omnipotent; let him be felt everywhere but not be seen.)

Joyce was to take this a little further:

The artist, like the God of creation, remains within or behind or beyond or above his handiwork, invisible, refined out of existence, indifferent, paring his finger nails.

(*A Portrait of the Artist as a Young Man*, London, 1950, p. 245)

Thomas Mann in several places speaks of God, the artist, and the

D

ironist in terms of one another. In *Lotte in Weimar*, for example, we are told that God's 'attitude is one of all-embracing irony'. His gaze 'is the gaze of absolute art, which is at once absolute love and absolute nihilism and indifference'. And in *Tonio Kröger*:

> [The curse of literature] begins by your feeling yourself set apart, in a curious sort of opposition to the nice, regular people; there is a gulf of ironic sensibility, of knowledge, scepticism, disagreement, between you and the others.
>
> (Trans. H. T. Lowe-Porter, London, 1955, pp. 113 – 14)

Excursus on the ironies of the theatre

The list of major ironists in Chapter 1, pp. 2–3 provided evidence of a strong link between irony and drama or the theatre. We may now be in a position to see what reasons there are for this link, that is to say, whether the nature of drama in the theatre is such that dramatists tend to introduce irony. We are arguing here as a man would argue who says that the nature of marble (as compared with wood, bronze, etc.) is such that sculptures in marble tend to have certain qualities and that, while the sculptor is free to make as little of the possibilities inherent in his medium as he pleases, he will be more likely to make a good deal of them.

The *données* of drama in the theatre seem to be these:

1. The facts of authorship and production.
2. The facts of presentation:
   (a) a real place – the stage (and the theatre generally);
   (b) a real time, restricted and uninterrupted – the time of enactment;
   (c) real flesh and blood in action – the actors.
3. An impersonation and enactment.
4. The facts of spectatorship.
5. The fact of repetition of performance.
6. An action – the story that is enacted.

If we group 1–5 together and call them the conditions or circumstances under or in which the action or story is enacted, we can see that 1–5 and 6 exist on two quite separate levels. The world of Gottlieb and Babette Biedermann, for example, knows nothing of Max Frisch who wrote *Biedermann und die Brandstifter*, nor of Lindsay Anderson who produced it at the Royal Court Theatre on 21 December 1961, nor of Alfred Marks who took the leading role, nor of Sir Joseph and Lady Blow in the audience who preferred Oskar Wälterlin's Zürich production.

Strictly speaking, it makes as little sense to say that Hamlet is unaware of being 'in *Hamlet*' as to say that the daughters of Leucippus are unaware of being in Rubens' painting of their abduction. But because the Hamlets we see are embodied in actual men whom we see moving and hear talking, it is very easy to think of them as being unaware of their status as actors. If it were not, we should not find Shakespeare exploiting the comic potential of this by giving an actor words which imply that he is unaware of being in England:

> TRINCULO [seeing Caliban]: What have we here? a man or a fish?
> ... A strange fish! Were I in England now, as once I was, and had
> but this fish painted, not a holiday fool there but would give a
> piece of silver: there would this monster make a man; any strange
> beast there makes a man.
>
> (*The Tempest*, II, ii)

According to Sedgewick this unawareness of the characters constitutes in itself an ironic situation which he calls 'general dramatic irony':

> The very theatre itself, I suggest to you, is a sort of ironic convention
> whereby a spectator occupying a good seat, as it were, in the real
> world is enabled to look into a world of illusion and so to get 'a view
> of life from on high'. And no pleasure, say Lucretius and Bacon, is
> comparable to that. A phrase long ago hackneyed by the text-book
> maker describes the stage as a room with the fourth wall down. Stale

as the image seems, there may be sap in it yet. The people living in that room behave with an utter unconsciousness that anyone is spying on them. Worse than that, for them at least, the spy comes to learn and know far more about them than they ever know themselves. . . . The peculiar pleasure of the theatre, then, is the spectacle of a life in which, it is true, we do not interfere but over which we exercise the control of knowledge. And this spectacle, when it pleases or holds us, we do not view with the 'swelling or pride' of superiority but with a sort of paradoxical sympathy; for, though it is *sympathy,* it is likewise *detached.* . . . *The whole attitude of the interested spectator is ironic;* by the very fact that he is such a spectator, he is an ironist.

(*Of Irony, Especially in Drama,* pp. 32–33)

It might be better to regard this not as irony, since we are not continually aware in the theatre of the characters' unawareness, but as a potentially ironic situation capable of being actualized at any time and in several ways. A character's unawareness of being, as a role or an actor, subjected to a dramatist or producer may be actualized as irony in a rehearsal play or a play about a play. Such plays are to be found as early as Beaumont and Fletcher's *Knight of the Burning Pestle* and as late as Peter Weiss's *Marat/Sade;* there were as many as sixty-five plays of this kind produced in England between 1671 and 1738. The irony of a character's not knowing that his actions are being manipulated by another character or being unable to prevent it is not uncommon in the theatre; Iago, Prospero, the Duke in *Measure for Measure,* Mosca in *Volpone,* De Flores in *The Changeling,* Dorante in *Le bourgeois gentilhomme,* Ibsen's Hedda Gabler, Hugo in Anouilh's *Ring Around the Moon,* Eliot's Harcourt-Reilly, are all directing intelligences masterminding the action and can all be seen as 'internalizations' of the facts of authorship, production, and stage-managing.

In so far as irony involves an appearance contrasting with a reality, it is potential in the very fact of impersonation. Nothing could be more common in the theatre than ironies of mistaken identity. Not knowing who or what one is, finding out one's parentage, passing oneself off or being passed off or accepted as someone else, whether by dressing-up or not, being unmasked, stripping off one's disguise or one's pretences: all of this can be seen as an 'internalization' of the fact that actors impersonate characters for a time and then resume their ordinary appearances.

The irony of being unaware that the real situation is very different from what it seems to be is equally common. Dramatic irony is more striking when the audience's superior knowledge is shared by one or more characters and particularly when the victim is unaware of the presence of such characters on the stage. Britannicus, not knowing that Néron is listening to his conversation with Junie, is in a situation repeated as to essentials in a hundred plays, comedies as well as tragedies. The particular force of such a situation may derive from the fact that it is a doubling of the spectator's role of the unobserved observer.

It is ironic when a character shows a confidence in the future if the audience already knows how black the future will be. We see Duncan, serenely unsuspicious, walking towards his death:

> This castle hath a pleasant seat: the air
> Nimbly and sweetly recommends itself
> Unto our gentle senses.
> . . . .
> Conduct me to mine host: we love him highly,
> And shall continue our graces towards him.
>
> *(Macbeth,* I, vi)

There is no obligation upon a dramatist to give the audience a foreknowledge of events. On the other hand a play seems by its nature to be something that one goes to see again and again, whereas a novel is *on the whole* something one has not read before. In any case it is easier to get to know the story of a play even before seeing it for the first time, and this will encourage a dramatist to prefer dramatic irony to surprise.

There are, however, further considerations which the nature of drama suggests. Whereas a novel tends to relate, in the past tense, actions already completed, a play presents an action being fulfilled. A novel, offering itself to the reader, says in effect, 'Let me tell you how it all happened'; a play says, 'Watch what is going to happen.' This is not to suggest that plays or even tragedies are typically heavy with fate and prophecies to be fulfilled, but only that the freewill of dramatic characters seems to be more circumscribed. The relative brevity of plays and consequently the greater economy and tightness of construction is probably an additional factor in keeping the flesh-and-blood character in touch with his humbler relation the marionette. The fact that one can close a book or switch off a radio has been 'internalized' in the form of chapters and 'serials'; the fact that one cannot stop a play may also be internally reflected as part of the sense of an inevitable working-out of events.

The argument, to sum up the last few pages, is that in drama the characters' necessary 'ignorance' of dramatist, producer, actor, plot, and audience constitutes a potential irony and a standing invitation to dramatists to actualize it. The nature of the total theatrical situation seems to prompt certain 'internalizations', the effect in each case being to make the character a victim of irony and the spectator an ironic observer. There is a pleasure in watching people who are unaware of being seen; there is a greater pleasure, and often a painful one, in watching people who are also unaware of the predicament they are in or are about to be in. The greater the contrast between, on the one hand, the victim's confident assumption that he is a free agent and that things will happen as he expects them to and, on the other, the spectator's view of him as a blind wretch fixed to the wheel of an irreversible, unstoppable action, the more intense the irony. There is hardly a dramatist who does not in some degree exploit this potential for dramatic irony by giving his audience a superior knowledge to match their, theatrically speaking, superior position.

We need to add at this point that although irony achieves its most striking effects in the theatre the range of effects is comparatively limited. It is to the novel that we must turn for more subtle and more complex ironies. In part, this is simply a function of the novel's greater length; the novelist, having more room to manœuvre in, can develop in detail the inner life of his characters and contrast this with the outer world of events. But the novel has the possibility of subsisting at an additional level, that of the authorial commentary, and consequently has the possibility of contrasting the author's point of view with that he gives his characters. There may also be, as in Thomas Mann's *Doctor Faustus*, a narrator whose point of view is not necessarily that of the author. The element of detachment is obvious in such cases.

The aesthetic element

There is one more 'basic feature' I should like to see incorporated into any general account of irony, and that is an aesthetic quality. We can see easily enough that Verbal Irony if not always an art always has an aesthetic element. Just as a funny story with all the proper ingredients will not amuse us if badly told, so irony, if it is not to be ineffective, has to be 'shaped'. The art of irony, in its slighter manifestations, resembles that of the wit or the raconteur, which relies largely upon arranging, timing, and tone, and it does not abandon these cares as it grows more ambitious. Stylistically speaking, irony is dandyism, whose first aim, as Max Beerbohm, ironist and dandy, tells us, is 'the production of the supreme effect through means the least extravagant'.

The ironic events and situations which life itself presents are likewise more or less effective according as they exhibit the balance, economy, and precision of a work of art. They fall into the category of *objets trouvés*, in that they look as if the chance that made them had an artistic sensibility. As Aristotle says:

> We find that, among events merely casual, those are the most wonderful and striking which seem to imply design: as when, for instance, the statue of Mitys at Argos killed the very man who had murdered Mitys, by falling down upon him as he was surveying it; events of this kind not having the appearance of an accident.
>
> (*Poetics*, 1452a)

The irony of the robber robbed is more striking if the robbing and the being robbed are simultaneous as in our example of the pickpocket or if the robber is paid in his own coin which is also the case here. But the irony of a pickpocket merely having his house burgled is less striking.

We must now ask whether it is not misleading to say that life presents ironic events and situations. People who write on irony usually take their examples of Situational Irony from literature, which is to say that their examples are inventions. And this is frequently true also of examples purporting to be from life, as in the case of the pickpocket. And even when the examples are really taken from life they are presented by someone who has consciously or unconsciously shaped the incident in his mind, cutting out irrelevancies, sharpening the contrasts, bringing incongruous elements into closer relationship, or heightening the confident unawareness of the victim. It is not inconceivable that on some occasion a fire-engine, gleaming with efficiency, has arrived just as the last wall of the burning house collapsed and has been greeted with ironical cheers. But it is far more likely that someone would invent such an incident to exemplify an ironic event. According to Kierkegaard, Situational Irony

> is not present in nature for one who is too natural and too naïve, but only exhibits itself for one who is himself ironically developed. Schubert . . . calls attention to the fact that nature has ironically juxtaposed the most remote extremes: 'Following immediately after

the rational and moderate human being – in the free association of ideas of natural species – comes the absurd ape, . . .' Now all such features are not in nature, but the ironic subject perceives them in nature. Similarly, one may also regard every deception of the senses as an irony of nature. But to become conscious of this requires a consciousness which is itself ironical. Indeed, the more polemically developed an individual is, the more irony he will find in nature. Such a view of nature belongs, therefore, more to the romantic than the classical development.

(Concept of Irony, pp. 271–2)

A sense of irony involves not only the ability to see ironic contrasts but also the power to shape them in one's mind. It includes the ability, when confronted with anything at all, to imagine or recall or notice something which would form an ironic contrast. Matthew Arnold, for example, faced with the 'exuberant self-satisfaction' of Sir Charles Adderley and Mr Roebuck saying:

'Such a race of people as we stand, so superior to all the world! The old Anglo-Saxon race, the best breed in the whole world! I pray that our unrivalled happiness may last! I ask you whether, the world over or in past history, there is anything like it?'

confronts it with a paragraph he came across by chance in a newspaper:

A shocking child murder has just been committed at Nottingham. A girl named Wragg left the workhouse there on Saturday morning with her young illegitimate child. The child was soon afterwards found dead on Mapperly Hills, having been strangled. Wragg is in custody.

(Essays in Criticism, 'The Function of Criticism at the Present Time')

The effect, as was intended, is that of an ironic contrast. Chance provided Arnold only with the possibility of bringing into ironic juxtaposition a complacent and a disturbing picture of nineteenth-century England; it was Arnold's sense of irony which brought them together, so constituting an ironic situation. Similarly, Arnold's incidental comment on the ugliness of the name 'Wragg' – 'In Ionia and Attica they were luckier in this respect . . . by the Ilissus there was no Wragg, poor thing!' – can be given an ironic connotation at Arnold's expense by recalling that infanticide was not unknown in Attica and that Plato even recommended it (in certain circumstances) for his ideal republic.

The 'basic features' we have now presented are these: a confident unawareness (real or pretended), a contrast of appearance and reality, a comic element, an element of detachment, and an aesthetic element. In view of such passages as this from Thomas Mann:

> The novel . . . keeps its distance from things, *has* by its very nature distance from them; it hovers over them and smiles down upon them, regardless of how much, at the same time, it involves the hearer or reader in them by a process of weblike entanglement. The art of the epic is 'Apollinian' art as the aesthetic term would have it; because Apollo, distant marksman, is the god of distance, of objectivity, the god of irony. Objectivity is irony and the spirit of epic art is the spirit of irony,
>
> (Thomas Mann, The Art of the Novel, p. 88)

it seems possible that further consideration might find some way of grouping together the element of detachment and the comic and aesthetic elements. It is at any rate clear that they overlap.

3
On Being Ironical

The distinction between Verbal Irony and Situational Irony is generally, though not universally, accepted. The former is the irony of an ironist being ironical; the latter is the irony of a state of affairs or an event seen as ironic. Situational Irony, I have argued, is perhaps only rarely found 'in a natural state'; that is to say, the people who see things as ironic are those whose sense of irony enables them mentally to 'construct' an ironic state of affairs out of 'raw material' (by excluding what might obscure or lessen the victim's confident unawareness or diminish the contrast of reality and appearance) and so give aesthetic shape to the untidiness of life.

The term 'Verbal Irony' is unsatisfactory since the ironist may use other media. One can bow or smile ironically, paint ironical pictures, or compose ironical music. But since the aim of all 'Behavioural Irony', whatever medium is employed, is to convey a meaning, this kind of irony is still to be regarded as 'linguistic'. In the Tartuffe painting described in Chapter 1, the devotional attitude and the lady's garter are both 'signs'; and a parody of, say, Baroque music would consist of exaggerated examples of the musical conventions or stylistic procedures that operate as signs of the Baroque. With Situational Irony, on the other hand, although there is also a revelation of a reality behind an appearance, no meaning is conveyed; the revealed reality is a state of affairs, not a proposition, and can be given meaning only by an observer.

The presentation of Situational Irony in literature complicates this. An ironist can praise a man for piety, letting it be understood that this praise is to be construed as an attack upon a religious hypocrite. Alternatively, he can invent and present a religious hypocrite behaving piously but unintentionally revealing his true nature. In this case a character embodies the pretended opinion of an ironist who is being ironical by presenting an ironic situation. There are also instances of a sort of fusion between straight Verbal Irony and this 'presented' Situational Irony: a character's thoughts are expressed partly in the ironist's words and partly in the words the victim himself might have used. An example will be clearer than a description. Here is Lytton Strachey presenting Florence Nightingale in later life:

> With statesmen and governors at her beck and call, with her hands on a hundred strings, with mighty provinces at her feet, with foreign governments agog for her counsel, building hospitals, training nurses – she still felt that she had not enough to do. She sighed for more worlds to conquer – more, and yet more. She looked about her – what was there left? Of course! Philosophy! After the world of action, the world of thought. Having set right the health of the British Army, she would now do the same good service for the religious convictions of mankind. She had long noticed – with regret – the growing tendency towards free-thinking among artisans. With regret, but not altogether with surprise: the current teaching of Christianity was sadly to seek; nay, Christianity itself was not without its defects. She would rectify these errors. She would correct the mistakes of the Churches; she would point out just where Christianity was wrong; and she would explain to the artisans what the facts of the case really were.
>
> (*Eminent Victorians*, London, 1928, pp. 105–06)

The two kinds nevertheless remain distinct. It is a distinction we make every day when we say of one kind, He is being ironical, and of the other, Isn't that ironic? The distinction, moreover, is maintained in academic discussion: Verbal Irony raises questions that come under the headings of rhetoric, stylistics, narrative and satiric forms, satiric strategies; Situational Irony, while raising fewer formal points, tends to raise historical and ideological questions – Who first saw *that* sort of thing as ironic? What sort of things do we regard as ironic? What sort of things are presented as ironic in Kafka, in Pirandello, in Proust? We look at Verbal Irony from the ironist's point of view but at Situational Irony from the ironic observer's point of view. Verbal Irony tends to be satiric; Situational Irony tends to be more purely comic, tragic, or 'philosophic'. We shall now look at some of the ways of being ironical.

SARCASM

It is questionable whether sarcasm is a form of irony. If it is a basic requirement of irony that we must feel the force of both the apparent and the real meanings, then sarcasm hardly exists as irony. The sarcast's tone so unequivocally conveys his real meaning that there can be scarcely any pretence of being unaware of it. None the less, the effect of sarcasm is not the same as the effect of direct language. Notice, however, in the example which follows how the direct 'Foolish soul!' can be placed without incongruity between two indirect sarcastic sentences. Carlyle's Teufelsdröckh is asking himself:

> What is this that, ever since earliest years, thou hast been fretting and fuming, and lamenting and self-tormenting, on account of? Say it in a word: is it not because thou art not HAPPY? Because the THOU (sweet gentleman) is not sufficiently honoured, nourished, soft-bedded, and lovingly cared-for? Foolish soul! What Act of Legislature was there that *thou* shouldst be Happy!
>
> (*Sartor Resartus*, Book II, Chapter IX)

Without implying that sarcasm has no legitimate function in oratory or literature (clearly there are occasions when the crudeness of sarcasm is the polemicist's most effective weapon; and crudeness may be employed with a high degree of art, as Milton's prose will show), we can still say that the art of sarcasm is barely related to the art of irony.

IMPERSONAL IRONY

I use this term for that way of being ironical which does not rely upon any weight being given to the ironist's personality. Most Verbal Irony is of this kind.

> The average man . . . believes that the text of ancient authors is generally sound, not because he has acquainted himself with the elements of the problem, but because he would feel uncomfortable if he did not believe it; just as he believes, on the same cogent evidence, that he is a fine fellow, and that he will rise again from the dead.
>
> (A. E. Housman, *Selected Prose*, Cambridge, 1961, p. 43)

Irony in this mode is normally characterized by a dryness or gravity of manner; the tone is that of a rational, casual, matter-of-fact, modest, unemotional speaker. Understatement, consequently, is a frequent form of impersonal irony; Kierkegaard presents the obviously absurd as the very slightly doubtful:

> Dear Reader: I wonder if you may not sometimes have felt inclined to doubt a little the correctness of the familiar philosophic [Hegelian] maxim that the external is the internal, and the internal the external.
>
> (*Either/Or*, trans. David and Lillian Swenson, New York, 1959, p. 3)

Some irony is meant to be seen through almost immediately; such overt irony need not be as obvious as sarcasm but it will be such as he that runs may read:

> Audiences are prepared to accept poetry recited by a chorus, for that is a kind of poetry recital, which it does them credit to enjoy.
>
> (T. S. Eliot, 'Poetry and Drama')

Some irony is meant rather to be detected; the half-concealment is part of the ironist's artistic purpose and the detection and appreciation of the camouflage is a large part of the reader's pleasure. This covert irony is frequent in Gibbon, especially in those places in which he pretends that his sympathies are with the ordinary unthinking Christian; we can imagine such a one reading the following passage and being now pleased by the author's apparent piety, now puzzled by his apparent support of the most questionable parts of the Holy Scriptures:

> There are some objections against the authority of Moses and the prophets which too readily present themselves to the sceptical mind; though they can only be derived from our ignorance of remote antiquity, and from our incapacity to form an adequate judgement of the Divine economy. These objections were eagerly embraced and as petulantly urged by the vain science of the Gnostics. As those heretics were, for the most part, averse to the pleasures of sense, they morosely arraigned the polygamy of the patriarchs, the gallantries of David, and the seraglio of Solomon. The conquest of the land of Canaan, and the extirpation of the unsuspecting natives, they were at a loss how to reconcile with the common notions of humanity and justice. But when they recollected the sanguinary list of murders, of executions, and of massacres, which stain almost every page of the Jewish annals, they acknowledged that the barbarians of Palestine had exercised as much compassion towards their idolatrous enemies as they had ever shown to their friends or countrymen.
>
> (*The Decline and Fall of the Roman Empire*, Chapter XV)

Samuel Butler's irony in his *Fair Haven* (1873) was even more covert. He published the work under a pseudonym and if he did not actually intend to be too subtle for the ordinary pious Christian of his time, he was delighted to discover that several reviewers took his ironical defence of Christian orthodoxy at face value. In the preface to the second edition Butler quotes from two reviews:

> [Written] throughout in downright almost pathetic earnestness.
>
> Mr Owen's exposition . . . is most admirable, and all should read it

who desire to know exactly what excuses men make for their incredulity. The work also contains many beautiful passages on the discomfort of unbelief, and the holy pleasure of a settled faith, which cannot fail to benefit the reader.

Kierkegaard goes so far as to claim that true irony (as distinct from rhetorical irony) 'does not generally wish to be understood' (*Concept of Irony*, p. 266).

This, of course, raises the question of how we recognize irony. We will be unable to recognize it (*a*) if the topic is controversial – a work called *In Praise of Folly* will be ironical but one called *In Praise of Older Women* need not be, (*b*) if we have no prior information about the writer or his views, and (*c*) if there are no clues in the text itself. This is often the case with letters to the editor, which, moreover, are not always written by practised writers: what looks very like a rationalizing, prejudiced, self-contradictory, inept defence of easier divorce may be precisely that and not ironical at all. Similarly, a novelist, writing in the convention of the impersonal author, presents without authorial comment a character whose actions and ideas the reader is supposed to find ridiculous. But the reader may not find them ridiculous, or, if he does, cannot know that the 'silent' author agrees with him. To this day people are uncertain whether Joyce was ironizing the hero of *The Portrait of the Artist as a Young Man* or presenting him for our admiration, or sometimes one and sometimes the other. This problem is treated at length in the last three chapters of Wayne C. Booth's *Rhetoric of Fiction*.

If a contrast of an appearance and a reality is a basic feature of irony, an awareness of contrast is a necessary condition of the recognition of irony. In Verbal Irony the contrast may be a contrast of text and context; the written statement 'I'm very fond of George' can be ironical only if contradicted by the context of facts and can be recognized as ironical only by those who know the facts. Or the contrast may be within the text:

Of the three popes, John the Twenty-third was the first victim: he fled and was brought back a prisoner: the most scandalous charges were suppressed; the vicar of Christ was only accused of piracy, murder, rape, sodomy and incest.

(Gibbon, *Decline and Fall of the Roman Empire*, Chapter LXX)

Perhaps most frequently the text is contradicted by the context but is also self-contradictory or at least contains some exaggeration, innuendo, ambiguity, or other stylistic warning signal:

The captain was now interred, and might, perhaps, have already made a large progress towards oblivion, had not the friendship of Mr Allworthy taken care to preserve his memory by the following epitaph which was written by a man of as great genius as integrity, and one who perfectly well knew the captain.

[This, while seeming to the careless reader to be no more flattering than the average epitaph, claims that Captain Blifil did the world an honour by condescending to exist.]

(Fielding, *The History of Tom Jones*, Book II, Chapter 9)

A person who has not read *Tom Jones* and does not perfectly well know the captain might not see this as ironical; nevertheless the contrast of text and context is supported by understatement – 'might, perhaps, have . . . made a large progress towards' – by ambiguity – 'as great genius as integrity' – and by exaggeration – the epitaph itself.

Contradictions may of course be accidental. In *Richard II*, Act V, Scene i, we read:

Northumberland, thou ladder wherewithal
The mounting Bolingbroke ascends my throne, . . .

In *Henry IV, Part II*, Act III, Scene i, Bolingbroke, now King Henry, says:

But which of you was by —
You, cousin Nevil, as I may remember —
When Richard, with his eye brimful of tears,

> Then check'd and rated by Northumberland,
> Did speak these words, . . .
> 'Northumberland, thou ladder by the which
> My cousin Bolingbroke ascends my throne;'
> (Though then, God knows, I had no such intent, . . .)

There are several contradictions here: the quotation is amended – in Bolingbroke's favour; the words were originally spoken, as God doubtless knows, *after* Richard has been deposed by Bolingbroke; and neither Bolingbroke nor 'cousin Nevil' was present to hear Richard's words. We might add that Henry IV has just been complaining of Northumberland's treachery first to Richard and then to him, but, naturally, has not mentioned his own treachery. The reader has to balance the probability of Shakespeare's being ironical against the probability of Shakespeare's having mistaken the context of Richard's speech (it could well have come from Act III, Scene iii), and there seems to be no way of reaching a decision. There is a similar problem in *Paradise Lost*: Eve claims to have overheard Raphael warning Adam against Satan at a time when she could only have overheard him warning Adam against her. Was Milton being careless or, in view of a later identification of Eve and the serpent, ironical?

SELF-DISPARAGING IRONY

The 'impersonal' ironist conceals himself behind a mask: his words alone, or their contrast with what we already know, effect the irony. In self-disparaging irony the ironist also wears a mask, but it is a mask which functions positively as a disguise or *persona*. The ironist brings himself on stage, so to speak, in the character of an ignorant, credulous, earnest, or over-enthusiastic person. Where the 'impersonal' ironist may practise verbal understatement, the self-disparaging ironist understates himself, and the impression he gives of himself is part of his ironic strategy. This is the principal ironical technique of Socrates whom Plato presents as the sort of person who sits admiringly at the feet of wise men eager to learn at last the nature of virtue, justice, and holiness, and as the sort of person who can only understand things at his own low level by the painful process of simple, obvious questions which can be answered with a Yes or No. It is the irony of Chaucer who presents himself as slow on the uptake, socially clumsy, a bookworm knowing nothing of love or life, a mere versifier unable fully to understand the stories he is turning into English. It is the irony of Pascal in the *Provinciales* who presents himself as an earnest seeker after truth painfully striving to make sense of what seem to his limited understanding to be (in the theological arguments of the anti-Jansenists) meaningless words, equivocations, or distinctions without a difference:

> Ce mot me fut nouveau, & inconnu. Jusques-là j'avois entendu les affaires; mais ce terme me jetta dans l'obscurité, & je croy qu'il n'a esté inventé que pour broüiller. Je luy en demanday donc l'explication; mais il m'en fit un mystere, & me renvoya, . . . Je chargeai ma memoire de ce terme. Car mon intelligence n'y avoit aucune part. Et, de peur de l'oublier je fus promptement retrouver mon Janseniste.

> (This word was new and strange to me. So far I had understood things; but this term plunged me in the dark, and I quite think it was invented only to spread confusion. I asked him therefore to explain it but he made a mystery of it and sent me off. . . . I charged my memory with this word; for my understanding had no part in it. And for fear of forgetting it I made haste to find my Jansenist again.)
> (*Provincial Letters*, First Letter)

INGÉNU IRONY

Self-disparaging Irony shades off into another mode in which the ironist, instead of presenting *himself* as a simpleton, puts forward in his place a simpleton or *ingénu* who is to be regarded as distinct from the ironist. The stalking-horse is replaced by the decoy-duck, which brings the ironist's victims into range but is quite unaware of its function. The *ingénu* may ask questions or make comments the full import of which he does not realize. The effectiveness of this ironical mode comes from its economy of means; mere common sense or even simple innocence or ignorance may suffice to cut through the complexities of hypocrisy or expose the irrationality of prejudice. The following example comes from a rather third-rate sketch of Mark Twain's, *Little Bessie Would Assist Providence:*

> 'Mama, why is there so much pain and sorrow and suffering? What is it all for? . . .'
> 'It is for our good, my child. In His wisdom and mercy the Lord sends us these afflictions to discipline us and make us better. . . . None of them comes by accident. . . .'
> 'Isn't it strange? . . . Did He give Billy Norris the typhus?'
> 'Yes.'
> 'What for?'
> 'Why, to discipline him and make him good.'
> 'But he died, mama, and so it couldn't make him good.'
> 'Well, then, I suppose it was for some other reason. . . . I think it was to discipline his parents.'
> 'Well, then, it wasn't fair, mama. . . . *he* was the one that was punished. . . . Did He make the roof fall in on the stranger that was trying to save the crippled old woman from the fire, mama?'

(Quoted from Norman Foerster, ed., *American Poetry and Prose*, 4th edn., Boston, 1957, pp. 1048–49)

IRONY OF SELF-BETRAYAL

An impersonal ironist says something in such a way or in such a context that his audience apprehends the real meaning of his words. A self-disparaging ironist presents himself as less intelligent than his interlocutor and does it in such a way that the pretensions of the latter are exposed. In *Ingénu* Irony the 'fictionalization' is carried further, a simpleton is created who is not the ironist, although, without knowing it, he acts on his behalf. The next step in the evolution of ironic strategies is for the ironist to withdraw completely and to create characters who unconsciously ironize themselves. It is odd that this kind of irony has not been clearly identified until quite recently. So far as I know, the first writer explicitly to mention it was G. G. Sedgewick:

> There is no time to exhibit irony as a means of character revelation; but witness Malvolio, and the long line of more serious self-deceivers in Shakespeare, like Brutus and Antony.
>
> *(Of Irony*, p. 30, first edition, 1935)

Eleanor Hutchens in her *Irony in* TOM JONES (p. 54) uses the term 'unconscious self-betrayal'.

A satirist who wishes to condemn a particular vice or folly can do it very effectively by putting a self-contradictory argument into the mouth of a would-be wise or virtuous character. Butler, wishing to ridicule the doctrine of Special Providence, makes the hero of *Erewhon* say after a narrow escape from drowning: 'As luck would have it, Providence was on my side.' A superb example may be found in Gottfried Keller's *Der grüne Heinrich* (1879): Keller tells a story of the persecution of a child by a hypocritical, sadistic, and self-seeking pastor who, unknown to himself, reveals these qualities in the journal he keeps. Space allows me only a brief quotation but long enough, I trust, to indicate its quality:

> Further, administered to the Child Meret (Emerentia) her weekly *Correction*, though more rigorous than before, laying her upon the Bench and applying a new Rod, not without Lamentation and Sighings to the Lord God, that He might bring this grievous Task to a good End.
>
> • • •
>
> Have changed my *Method* with the Child and will now essay the Hunger Cure. Have also caused my own Wife to make a Shift of coarse Sackcloth, and have forbidden Meret to wear any other Attire,

this penitential Shift being most suited to her. Stubbornness at the same *Puncto*.

Today was forced to prevent the little Demoiselle from all Association and Play with the Village Children, she having run with them into the Wood and there bathed in the Pool, hanging the penitential Shift I caused to be made for her on the Branch of a Tree and dancing before it naked, provoking even her Playmates to Impudence and Wantonness. Considerable *Correction*.

．　　．　　．

[A painter is engaged by the child's parents]

When we took out from the Chest the Dress and Sunday Finery of the Child, and put it on her with her Crown and Belt, she made show of great Pleasure and began to dance. But this her Joy soon turned to Bitterness when I, upon the order of her Lady Mamma, sent for 1 Skull and placed it in her Hand, she resisting with all her Might, and then holding it in her Hand weeping and trembling, as if it were glowing Iron. The Painter declared that he could paint the Skull by Heart, the same being one of the Elements of his Art, but I would not allow it, Madame having written: 'What the Child suffers, we suffer also, and in her Suffering lies our Opportunity of doing Penance, provided we do it for her Sake; for that reason we would have Your Reverence make no Change in your Care and Education. If, as I hope to the Almighty and Merciful God, the Child shall one Day receive Enlightenment at one Point or other and be saved, she will doubtless rejoice greatly that she has done with a great Deal of her Penance by her present Habit of Stubbornness, which Our inscrutable Lord has been pleased to afflict her with.'

The Irony of Self-betrayal is related both to Dramatic Irony, in which the victim is serenely unaware that the real state of affairs is quite different from what he assumes it is, and to the Irony of Events, in which what happens is the reverse of what is confidently expected. These two forms of irony are extremely common, especially in drama, but they do not offer as much scope for satiric irony as the kinds we have been discussing. The satiric point can only be that the victim is at most arrogantly blind or foolishly confident and this does not allow of much variation. We shall, however, return to these two ironies in the next chapter.

IRONY OF SIMPLE INCONGRUITY

We say it is ironic when two highly incongruous or incompatible phenomena are found in close juxtaposition as in the street name 'Impasse de l'Enfant Jésus'. And it is an ironical technique to juxtapose without comment two contradictory statements or incongruous images. We have seen Matthew Arnold juxtaposing complacent national pride and a disturbing workhouse tragedy. Pope, more economically, describes the clutter of Belinda's dressing-table:

> Puffs, Powders, Patches, Bibles, Billet-doux.

In *Madame Bovary* Flaubert presents simultaneously the agricultural fair at Yonville with its speeches and prizes and Rodolphe's well-worn line of love-talk, the one as banal as the other:

> From magnetism little by little Rodolphe had come to affinities, and while the president was citing Cincinnatus and his plough, Diocletian planting his cabbages, and the Emperors of China inaugurating the year by the sowing of seed, the young man was explaining to the young woman that these irresistible attractions find their cause in some previous state of existence.
>
> 'Thus we,' he said, 'why did we come to know one another? What chance willed it? It was because across the infinite, like two streams that flow but to unite, our special bents of mind had driven us towards each other.'
>
> And he seized her hand; she did not withdraw it.
>
> 'For good farming generally!' cried the president.
>
> 'Just now, for example, when I went to your house —'
>
> 'To Monsieur Bizat of Quincampoix —'
>
> 'Did I know I should accompany you?'

'Seventy francs.'

'A hundred times I wished to go; and I followed you – I remained.'
'Manures!'

'And I shall remain tonight, tomorrow, all other days, all my life!'
'To Monsieur Caron of Argueil, a gold medal!'

'For I have never in the society of any other person found so complete a charm.'

'To Monsieur Bain of Givry-Saint-Martin.'

'And I shall carry away with me the remembrance of you.'
'For a merino ram!'

(Part II, Chapter VIII)

4
On Seeing Things as Ironic

Verbal Irony is employed principally (i) as a rhetorical device –
the ironist asserts a 'falsehood' knowing he can rely upon the
listener to contradict it mentally by an indignant or amused
counter-assertion, this counter-assertion with all its emphasis
being the ironist's real meaning, (ii) as solemn foolery – Jane
Austen, in a youthful letter to her sister: 'I am very much flattered
by your commendation of my last letter, for I write only for fame,
and without any view to pecuniary emolument,' (iii) as a weapon
of satire, or, more broadly, in the interests of morality. As a
satirist or moralist, the ironist may, as we have seen, present
situational ironies, particularly ironies of self-betrayal or
incongruity.

It is probable that no one ever presents an ironic situation
without some kind of moral purpose; it is also probable that all
literature is moral, and the more likely this is to be true the less
interesting a truth it becomes. What seems more interesting is that
the irony of ironic situations can be presented for its own sake; for
an ironic observer the spectacle of irony, whether chiefly comic or
chiefly pathetic or tragi-comic, is a spectacle worth attending to.
Just as there is a special pleasure in 'interpreting' Verbal Irony, in
seeing in a set of words a meaning that 'literally' is not there at all
and a meaning, moreover, that contradicts the meaning that *is*
there, so there is a special pleasure in seeing someone serenely
unaware of being in a predicament, especially when this predicament is the contrary of the situation he assumes himself to be in.
It would be difficult to account for this pleasure in purely humani-
tarian terms. But, as we have already seen, the ironic observer is

in a special relationship to what he observes; he is detached from what he observes and this ironic spectacle has, as we have seen, an aesthetic quality which, so to speak, objectifies it. So that however much one may feel the poignancy of Othello's or Iphigenia's position, one also sees them as beings in another world, fixed and caught up in an action that denies them any freedom, while all the time they think they exercise it. We are reminded of Horace Walpole's saying: 'The world is a comedy to those that think, a tragedy to those that feel.'

DRAMATIC IRONY AND IRONY OF EVENTS

Dramatic irony, as we have seen, is the staple irony of the theatre. It is not, of course, confined to drama and we have already seen an instance in Homer – the suitors in the *Odyssey* expressing their confidence that Odysseus, who has already returned and is there in the hall disguised as a beggar, will never return. There are instances of dramatic irony in the Bible. Job does not know that he is the subject of a wager between God and Satan and that his misfortunes constitute steps in a scientific experiment not altogether unlike those modern experiments designed to see at what point a series of electric shocks will induce neuroses in rats. Joseph royally entertains his brothers in Egypt and they do not know that this great man is the brother they sold into slavery. Anglo-Saxon narrative poetry provides further instances: Judith, having killed Holofernes in his tent, returns with his head to the Hebrews who then sally out against the enemy. The captains of the hard-pressed Assyrians think they should report to Holofernes but being afraid to interrupt his pleasure only stand outside his tent and cough.

There is an excellent example in Euripides' *Iphigenia at Aulis*, powerful enough to stand up to a plain translation from a difficult text. Iphigenia thinks she has been brought to Aulis to be married

to Achilles; her father, Agamemnon, cannot bring himself to tell
her that at his command she has been brought there to be sacrificed:

IPHIGENIA: Father, O I am glad to see you after this long time.

AGAMEMNON: Yes, and your father to see you. What you say holds
true for both of us.

IPHIGENIA: You did well to have me brought to you, Father.

AGAMEMNON: That is something, child, I cannot confirm or deny.

IPHIGENIA: What is it? You looked troubled, for all your gladness
seeing me.

AGAMEMNON: A man has many worries when he is a king and
general.

. . .

IPHIGENIA: You are going on a long journey, Father, leaving me
behind.

AGAMEMNON: It is the same for both of us, daughter.

IPHIGENIA: Ah! If only it were right for me to sail with you!

AGAMEMNON: You have a voyage to make too and you will not
forget your father there.

IPHIGENIA: Will I sail with my mother, or alone?

AGAMEMNON: Alone, separated from father and mother.

IPHIGENIA: You are sending me away to a new home somewhere,
aren't you, Father?

AGAMEMNON: That is enough. Girls should not know such things.

IPHIGENIA: Please hurry back from Phrygia, Father, after victory
there.

AGAMEMNON: First I must offer sacrifice here.

IPHIGENIA: Yes, we must look to the proper performance of our
duty to the gods at any rate.

AGAMEMNON: You will see, for you will stand near the lustral
bowl.

IPHIGENIA: Then, I will lead the dance round the altar, Father.

Dramatic Irony seems more effective when not only the
audience or reader but also someone in the play or narrative is
aware of the victim's ignorance, as in this dialogue of Agamemnon
and Iphigenia. This can be complicated further when A and B

talk about C who is concealed, but only from B. Here A, C, and the audience are all aware of B's ignorance but each is in a different relationship to B. In Sheridan's *School for Scandal* there are two separately concealed characters. The effect of Dramatic Irony is greatly enhanced when the victim's words are, unknown to him, appropriate to the real situation he is unaware of. The most famous instance is doubtless Oedipus's curse upon himself:

> And it is my solemn prayer
> That the unknown murderer, and his accomplices,
> If such there be, may wear the brand of shame
> For their shameful act, unfriended, to their life's end.

The Irony of Self-betrayal, discussed in the last chapter, is not dissimilar to Dramatic Irony, the victim revealing self-ignorance, however, and not ignorance of the situation he is in. Closer to Dramatic Irony in this respect is the Irony of Events; the victim more or less explicitly expresses reliance on the future, but some unforeseen turn of events reverses and frustrates his plans, expectations, hopes, fears, or desires. He gets at last but too late what he once desired; he throws away what he later finds is indispensable; to reach a certain goal he takes unknowingly precisely the steps that lead him away from it; the means he takes to avoid something turn out to be the means of bringing it about. In Anatole France's *Thaïs*, a hermit, confident of the integrity of his own soul, sets out to convert a courtesan. In this he succeeds, only to discover that he no longer cares for Thaïs's soul, since in the meantime he too has been converted – to a vampire.

GENERAL IRONY

Ironic situations, we have seen, can be invented or presented by satirists whose object is to expose hypocrisy, wilful ignorance, pride, confident folly, rationalizing, or vanity. In such corrective or normative uses of irony, the victim to be exposed and dis-comfited is singled out; he is 'in the wrong' and, by contrast, those to whom he is exposed are 'in the right' or at least safe from this particular attack. This is not incompatible with the view that the victim of satire is a sort of scapegoat driven from society burdened with the guilt of all its members, provided the satirist's audience does not hold this view. Satire, of course, is possible only to the extent that there are established, commonly accepted values.

It is not, however, necessary that irony should be satirical and specific, singling out a victim who has offended against the *mores* of the community. Irony may be 'metaphysical' and general, the ironist seeing the whole of mankind as victims of an irony inherent in the human condition. A French critic, Georges Palante, puts it this way:

> The metaphysical principle of irony ... resides in the contradictions within our nature and also in the contradictions within the universe or God. The ironic attitude implies that there is in things a basic contra-diction, that is to say, from the point of view of our reason, a funda-mental and irremediable absurdity.
>
> ('L'ironie: étude psychologique', *Revue philosophique de la France et de l'étranger*, Feb. 1906, p. 153)

Kierkegaard writes:

> Irony in the eminent sense directs itself not against this or that particular existence but against the whole given actuality of a certain time and situation. . . . It is not this or that phenomenon but the totality of existence which it considers *sub specie ironiae*.
>
> (*The Concept of Irony*, p. 271)

A recent work, Glicksberg's *The Ironic Vision in Modern Literature* (The Hague, 1969), is entirely devoted to this kind of irony, the irony of a society in which there are few established, commonly accepted values.

The basis for General Irony lies in those contradictions,

apparently fundamental and irresolvable, that confront men when they speculate upon such topics as the origin and purpose of the universe, the certainty of death, the eventual extinction of all life, the impenetrability of the future, the conflicts between reason, emotion, and instinct, freewill and determinism, the objective and the subjective, society and the individual, the absolute and the relative, the humane and the scientific. Most of these, it may be said, are reducible to one great incongruity, the appearance of self-valued and subjectively free but temporally finite egos in a universe that seems to be utterly alien, utterly purposeless, completely deterministic, and incomprehensibly vast. The universe appears to consist of two systems which simply do not gear together. The one functions, and can only function, in terms of meanings, values, rational choices, and purposes; the other seems not to be comprehensible in these terms. And yet, though the two systems are incompatible, they are also interinvolved; the alien system extends its dominance into the very centre of the 'human' system and the 'human' system feels obliged to find meanings, values, and purposes in the non-human, in short to reduce the duality to a unity.

One has to add here that this picture of the world may be quite wrong. It is, however, accepted as reality by a great many modern writers, and that is a sufficient basis for irony: the ironist needs only to be convinced that his view of reality is valid and another, contrary view is not. In this case the contrary view is the conviction that 'God's in his heaven – All's right with the world!' or at least an ineradicable feeling that the world really ought to make sense, that it ought to be organized according to the principles of reason and justice, that death is not really the end, that we do have freewill, that the rights of society and the individual are reconcilable, that man is not a biological dead-end, that life is not a chemical accident.

One has also to add that General Irony is an irony of a rather special kind, in that the ironic observer is also among the victims of irony along with the rest of mankind. As a result there is a tendency for General Irony to be presented as much from the point of view of the involved victim (who cannot help feeling that the universe really ought not to be quite so unfair in its dealings with men) as from the point of view of the detached observer. So that what is called World Irony or Philosophical Irony or Cosmic Irony is sometimes little more than a presentation of the helplessness of men in the face of an indifferent universe, a presentation coloured with feelings of resignation and melancholy or even despair, bitterness, and indignation. The 'cosmic belly-aching' of a Hardy at his worst is unhappily more typical than the vigorous intellectual control and *dégagé* manner of a Robert Musil.

It is probable that the perception of 'General Irony' situations is as old as philosophic thought, as old as the discovery that natural forces are not to be controlled by magic or propitiated by sacrifices. Historically speaking, General Irony appears in classical antiquity; it may already be inherent in the observation of Xenophanes (fifth or sixth century B.C.) that men make gods after their own image and that if horses had hands to fashion works of art their gods would be horselike. Anyone not familiar with the Greek mind would, however, be rash to assert the presence of General Irony even in those Greek plays in which man is shown as helpless in the face of blind fate or cruel gods. The following passages are perhaps as close as anything else in Greek drama to General Irony:

> Let all men here forgive me,
> And mark the malevolence
> Of the unforgiving gods
> In this event. We call them
> Fathers of sons, and they
> Look down unmoved
> Upon our tragedies.

The future is hidden from us.
This is the present —
Our grief, who see it;
His [Herakles'] untold agony,
Who must endure it;
And their reproach,
Who let it be.

Women of Trachis, you have leave to go.
You have seen strange things,
The awful hand of death, new shapes of woe,
Uncounted sufferings;
And all that you have seen
Is God.

(The close of Sophocles' *Women of Trachis*,
trans. E. F. Watling, Penguin, 1953)

. . . none can be called happy until that day
when he carries
His happiness down to the grave in peace.

(The last words of Sophocles' *Oedipus Rex*,
trans. E. F. Watling, Penguin, 1947)

With the denial by Christian theology of any radical conflict between man and Nature – man is Lord of Creation – or between man and God – man is the son of a loving Father – it is not surprising that General Irony does not appear in modern Europe until the closed world of the Christian ideology loses its power to convince. From the sixteenth century onwards, at first slowly and then with increasing speed, men became more and more aware of fundamental contradictions in life. This was the inevitable result, on the one hand, of the growth of the objective study of man and his world, and, on the other, of the growing reluctance both to obey such injunctions as 'Presume not God to scan' and to wait contentedly for the joys of heaven to compensate the evils of earthly existence.

Pascal did not hesitate to point out contradictions in the natural world but his object was to argue that these contradictions necessitate a supernatural solution. The incommensurability of man and Nature, which is both infinitely and incomprehensibly vast and infinitely and incomprehensibly small (or divisible), not only provides a necessary lesson in humility but also implies the existence of an infinite God who alone can comprehend infinity. But this is to beg the question, and Musil, on the same theme, ascribes man's ability to achieve a stable position not to God and a belief in Him but to a confidence-trick man plays upon himself:

By exercising great and manifold skill we manage to produce a dazzling deception by the aid of which we are capable of living alongside the most uncanny things and remaining perfectly calm about it, because we recognize these frozen grimaces of the universe as a table or a chair, a shout or an outstretched arm, a speed or a roast chicken. We are capable of living between one open chasm of the sky above our heads and one slightly camouflaged chasm of the sky beneath our feet, feeling ourselves as untroubled on the earth as in a room with the door locked. We know that life ebbs away both out into the inhuman distances of interstellar space and down into the inhuman construction of the atom-world; but in between there is a stratum of forms that we treat as the things that make up the world, without letting ourselves be in the least disturbed by the fact that this signifies nothing but a preference given to the sense-data received from a certain middle distance. Such an attitude lies considerably below the potentiality of our intellect, but precisely this proves that our feelings play a large part in all this. And in fact the most important intellectual devices produced by mankind serve the preservation of a constant state of mind, and all the emotions, all the passions in the world are a mere nothing compared to the vast but utterly unconscious effort that mankind makes in order to maintain its exalted peace of mind. It seems to be hardly worth while to speak of it, so perfectly does it function. But if one looks into it more closely one sees that it is nevertheless an extremely artificial state of mind that enables man to walk upright between the circling constellations and permits him, in the midst of the almost infinite *terra incognita* of the world around him, to place his hand with dignity between the second and third buttons of his coat.

(*The Man Without Qualities*, trans. Eithne Wilkins and Ernst Kaiser, London, 1961, Vol. II, pp. 275-6)

Perhaps the most convenient way to deal with General Irony will be to present a number of those aspects of life which seem most frequently to reveal 'fundamental contradictions'. There is, for example, a General Irony of Events based upon the certainty of death, the essential unpredictability of life in general, and the unbreakable chain of cause and effect. The irony of death is not simply that our objective conviction that we shall die is in radical opposition to our subjective refusal to believe it can really happen to us, which is the subject of Tolstoy's story *The Death of Ivan Ilyich*: there is a deeper irony in the view that it is precisely our absurd, indefensible rejection of death that enables us to go on living out our lives. An *effective* belief in our own mortality would entail an effective sense of the futility of life. Similarly with an effective belief in determinism or predestination or in the essential impenetrability of the future. Life is possible only within the illusion of freewill and only if we also assume a degree of reliability in the future. To leave everything to chance is to cut oneself completely adrift; to leave nothing to chance is the best way to become completely neurotic – and how does one determine how much to leave to chance? This irony has been explored exhaustively in Kafka's story *The Burrow*.

There is a General Irony again in the whole concept of progress. In one obvious sense – that of technological advance – progress is a fact; it would be hard to persuade an astronomer with access to a computer or the health authorities in a country which has eliminated smallpox or malaria that progress has not been made. They might, however, be open to the view that solving one problem is the surest means of discovering further unsuspected problems. Looking back, we can see how far we have come; but looking forward

> behold with strong Surprise
> New distant Scenes of *endless* Science rise.

Is an endless multiplication of problems really progress? Like the sorcerer's apprentice, knowing the magic spell but not the counter-spell, we have brought about a state of affairs that we can now do nothing about. Progress has got out of hand; having chosen to begin we cannot choose to stop and so we chase our own tail at ever-increasing speed. It is also ironic that progress has been and perhaps can only be on one plane. It is as if a man's hands, his manipulative organs, had become several times larger than the rest of his body and in growing had developed a mind and a will of their own. It is now the hands that, with a reversal of the usual embarrassing situation, do not know what to do with the man that is so awkwardly attached to them.

We call it Dramatic Irony when we see a man serenely unaware that the situation as he sees it is the contrary of the real situation. In so far as mankind is, in some respects, always and necessarily in such a predicament, he is a victim of a General Dramatic Irony. For example, it is recognized, at the speculative level, that men's actions are governed far more than they think by their genetic makeup, their climatic, national, and sociological environment, their childhood and later experiences, their physiological 'weather' that changes from hour to hour, their more constant biological drives, and their emotional states. And yet each of us thinks that, on the whole, he governs his life more rationally than otherwise, and that rationalizing is something indulged in only by other people.

Freudian psychology sees our conscious life as a façade behind which a very different 'real' life goes on in secret; our hidden fears and desires can ordinarily appear to consciousness only in disguised forms whose symbolism the psychoanalyst alone can decipher. The operations of the unconscious are described in terms similar to those we use when talking of irony: a man intends to say one thing but by a 'Freudian slip' he says something quite different and so reveals his real preoccupations, as in the Irony of Self-betrayal; artists through their unconscious 'choice' of subjects, motifs, or images, reveal meanings they did not intend; the concept of 'compensating' enables us to reverse the ostensible meaning of everything men say or do. In our conscious life we have all the 'innocent unawareness' of the typical victim of irony who assumes that things are what they appear to be. This makes us all unconscious hypocrites living a 'life of continuous and uninterrupted self-deception', as the Satanic angel in Mark Twain's *Mysterious Stranger* puts it. The things which we say happen to us against our will may really be the things which we secretly will to happen; the unconscious may have its reasons, which reason knows nothing of, for falling sick or into debt, for crashing the car or losing the job, or failing the examination.

General Irony becomes possible in another area with the raising of doubts about the purpose of life, and about the existence and nature of God and of the world beyond the world. Ironists, in the last two hundred years especially, have again and again realized this potential. This kind of irony can of course achieve very powerful effects because it can tap the enormous reservoir of emotions tied up in religious beliefs. For example, David Hume points out the uncertainties that arise if one tries to derive from the nature of Creation an adequate picture of the Creator:

This world, for aught [one] knows . . . was only the first rude essay of some infant deity who afterwards abandoned it, ashamed of his lame performance; it is the work only of some dependent, inferior deity, and is the object of derision to his superiors; it is the production of old age and dotage in some superannuated deity, and ever since his death has run on at adventures, from the first impulse and active force which it received from him.

(Dialogue Concerning Natural Religion, Part V)

Mark Twain in *The Mysterious Stranger* attempts to show that God's ways with men might well be Satan's. This is a reversion to a primitive way of regarding God, and Samuel Butler ironically explains our abandoning of it when he says that 'God and the Devil are an effort after specialization and division of labour' *(Notebooks,* London, 1918, p. 226). Hardy presents the Lord of the Universe sometimes as behaving towards his creatures as a cat towards a mouse, sometimes as a blind indifferent 'It' mechanically turning 'the handle of this idle show'.

We do not need to imagine either a malignant or an indifferent deity in order to see mankind as in an ironic predicament. Beckett presents the ironic absurdity of life by telescoping the life-span to a single instant:

POZZO: When! When! One day, is that not enough for you, one day like any other day, one day he went dumb, one day I went blind, one day we'll go deaf, one day we were born, one day we'll die, the same day, the same second, is that not enough for you? *(Calmer.)* They give birth astride of a grave, the light gleams an instant, then it's night once more.

VLADIMIR: ... Astride of a grave and a difficult birth. Down in the hole, lingeringly, the grave-digger puts on the forceps. We have time to grow old.

(Waiting for Godot, London, 1959, pp. 89, 91)

Samuel Butler does the same by looking at life from the quite different point of view provided by evolutionary theory:

A hen is only an egg's way of making another egg.

(Life and Habit, Chapter VIII)

Man is but a perambulating tool-box and workshop, or office, fashioned for itself by a piece of very clever slime, as a result of long experience; and truth is but its own most enlarged, general and enduring sense of the coming togetherness or con-venience of the various conventional arrangements which, for some reason or other, it has been led to sanction.

(The Notebooks, p. 18)

Beckett again, in *Endgame*, presents life as an unknowable, alien process in which we need not hope (or is it fear?) that mankind plays a meaningful role. Hamm and Clov are, apparently, the two last men on earth:

HAMM ... *(Anguished)*: Clov!
CLOV: Yes.
HAMM: What's happening?
CLOV: Something is taking its course.
  Pause
HAMM: Clov!
CLOV *(impatiently)*: What is it?
HAMM: We're not beginning to ... to ... mean something?
CLOV: Mean something! You and I, mean something!
(Brief laugh) Ah that's a good one!

(Endgame, London, 1958, pp. 26–27)

Kafka, in *The Trial*, presents the fact of human existence as a criminal offence, life as a trial (or the preliminaries to a trial) in which the defendant is utterly unable to find out the nature of the charge against him, and death as the execution of a sentence passed against him in his absence.

In the field of human knowledge there is wide scope for General Irony, since there is a fundamental contradiction between the desire to know everything and the impossibility of knowing everything. The desire to know everything has, at least in the Western world, been transformed into an obligation to know everything; one just has to go on finding out more and more about

King John's fiscal policy, verb phrase complements, and non-functional colouration in birds' eggs. 'Thou shalt not be ignorant' has been added to the Commandments. On the other hand, universal knowledge is impossible in several distinct respects. Astronomical knowledge of distant galaxies is necessarily hundreds of thousands of years out of date. We are told that it is statistically probable that these galaxies contain systems with planets inhabited by rational beings but we shall never be able to communicate with them because of this time-factor.

There is a General Irony in many other fundamental and unresolvable oppositions which life confronts us with and before which we can only say that there is much to be said for and against both sides. Every virtue has its vice, and every vice its virtue. Youth is a wonderful thing but it is wasted on the young, as Shaw said. We value stability and look for change; discipline is necessary – is freedom less so? We are both individuals and members of our society, needing to assert our independence and express our solidarity. The body is sometimes wiser than the mind, the heart a truer guide than the head; but these truths reason teaches. Take no thought for the morrow, but save for a rainy day. Be yourself, and mend your manners. Be moderate in all things, including moderation. For him who sees no possibility of reconciling such opposites the only alternative is irony: a sense of irony will not make him any the less a victim of these predicaments but will enable him in some degree to transcend them.

ROMANTIC IRONY

Literature too can be seen as a phenomenon containing contradictory or incompatible elements. A work of literature is both a communication and the thing communicated: it exists in the world and also sets itself apart from the world. It both draws attention to itself as art and pretends to be life. But, being static and finite, it is necessarily inadequate to the expression of the dynamic, whether this is its author's subjectivity or the infinite world. On the other hand, by its mere existence it gives clarity and form, meaning and value, to the mere existence it presents. Novalis defined irony as 'genuine consciousness, true presence of mind' (Wellek, p. 86). Romantic Irony (see also Chapter 2, pp. 20–21) is the irony of a writer conscious that literature can no longer be simply naïve and unreflective but must present itself as conscious of its contradictory, ambivalent nature. The author's 'presence of mind' must now be a principal element in his work, alongside the equally necessary but 'blind' driving force of enthusiasm or inspiration.

Ironic literature, in this sense of irony, is literature in which there is a constant dialectic interplay of objectivity and subjectivity, freedom and necessity, the appearance of life and the reality of art, the author immanent in every part of his work as its creative vivifying principle and transcending his work as its objective 'presenter'. Such literature, and the novel is the genre *par excellence* of Romantic Irony, subsists at two or more levels. To the writer the work at its 'lower' level is a game – a cat-and-mouse game with mice that the cat is really fascinated by and quite attached to. To the reader, whom the author takes into his confidence, the work has become a spectacle to observe with detached amusement as well as a story to be absorbed by; it is now one and now the other, like shot silk that can be both green and red or like the drawing of a cube that can be interpreted now as hollow and now as solid.

Romantic Irony is closely related to that ironic view of life expressed by Renan, 'The universe is a spectacle that God offers himself' (quoted from Chevalier, *The Ironic Temper*, pp. 46-47), and by others:

Nietzsche inherited from Schopenhauer the proposition that 'life as representation alone, seen pure or reproduced in art, is a significant spectacle' – the proposition, that is, that life can be justified only as an aesthetic phenomenon. Life is art and appearance, nothing more, and therefore wisdom (as an affair of culture and life) stands higher than truth (which is a matter of morality).

(Thomas Mann, 'Nietzsche's Philosophy in the Light of Recent History', trans. Richard and Clara Winston, in *Last Essays*, London, 1959, pp. 151–2)

Something like Romantic Irony (but it is only a first step towards it) may be found in works of all ages from Aristophanes to Evelyn Waugh or Raymond Queneau. In these works the author expresses his awareness that what he is writing is after all only an illusion by bringing himself or his readers unexpectedly into the work or, if it is a play, by making his actors drop their roles, or by ending a novel with the revelation that one of the characters is going to set about writing it, ending and all. We come closer to Romantic Irony when the work is accompanied by a critical commentary on events and characters and closer still when the commentary directs its ironic attention to literary composition in general or even to the composition of the work in hand. This is what the novel has offered us from its beginnings in *Don Quixote*, chiefly in the eighteenth century (Marivaux, Fielding, Sterne, Diderot, Goethe) but intermittently ever since.

The concept of Romantic Irony we owe principally to Friedrich Schlegel; Romantic Irony itself may be found in the plays of Ludwig Tieck, the stories of E. T. A. Hoffmann, the poetry of Heine, and, in its most fully developed form, the novels of Thomas Mann.

We can conclude both this section and our account of irony with a few brief observations on Thomas Mann's *Joseph and his Brothers* as a work written in the true spirit of Romantic Irony. The story of Joseph exists at several 'levels'. In the first place, a claim is entered, not seriously of course, for its existence as an historical event; but even at this level it is a story told by God to

o

Himself: God made things to happen as they did for the sake of their significance (a serious claim of exactly this kind lies behind the old allegorical or typological interpretations of the Old Testament). In the second place, the Joseph story is a myth and its many manifestations (in astrology, in Hebrew, Babylonian, Egyptian, and Greek mythology, in all stories both of substituted sacrifices and of death, descending to the Lower Kingdom and resurrection) point to an unchanging 'universal' structure supporting the 'particularity' of historical events. In the third place, there are several versions of the Joseph story (as story, not myth) and this raises novelistic questions concerning interpretation and the legitimacy and effect of abbreviation and expansion. And finally there is this latest version in which Joseph is presented as being aware of being in the 'God-story', of being a mythic hero, and of living a life which will be told as a story, and ironically aware, moreover, of his responsibilities to all three states. Thomas Mann presents all of this and shows himself too as ironically aware of his role as mythographer. Nor can we suppose him to have been other than continually aware of the ironic contrast between his restoration of a Hebrew myth and the contemporaneous restoration and perversion of Germanic mythology by the anti-semitic Nazis.

Thomas Mann said of the problem of irony that it was 'without exception the profoundest and most fascinating in the world'. From a figure of rhetoric, irony developed into the most sophisticated weapon at the disposal of satire, a development inseparable from the history of the art of prose. In another area, the history of irony is also the history of both comic and tragic awareness. In the last two hundred years, irony has enabled men to confront both the death of God and the discovery that the world was not made with them particularly in mind; and here nothing less is involved than the defeat of 'cosmic' hope and despair. Romantic Irony marks an important stage in literature, its coming to full consciousness of itself, 'the transition', in Merezhkovsky's words, 'from unconscious creation to creative consciousness', in Schiller's words from *naiv* to *sentimentalisch*, unreflective to reflective; art that holds the mirror up to Nature can now also hold a mirror up to the mirror of art.

Bibliography

The number of works in English which deal exclusively with the nature, concept, or history of irony is not large even if we include articles. There are even fewer in French, though many more in German. The most recent extensive bibliographies are in Hans-Egon Hass (comp.), *Ironie als Literarische Phanomen*, Koln, 1973 and Wayne C. Booth, *A Rhetoric of Irony*, Chicago, 1974. The number of articles on irony in individual authors or works is legion.

GENERAL WORKS IN ENGLISH INCLUDING TRANSLATIONS

COLLINS, A., *A Discourse Concerning Ridicule and Irony in Writing*, London, 1729.

'Its wide-ranging and exhaustive use of examples, the representative nature of its arguments, and the emphasis of its orientation make it a milestone in the history of general concern over irony.' (Knox)

THIRLWALL, C., 'On the Irony of Sophocles' in *The Philological Museum*, Vol. II, 1833, and in *Remains, Literary and Theological*, ed. J. Stewart Perowne, London, 1878, Vol. III.

There is a substantial summary of the theoretical part of this essay (essential for the history of the concept of irony) in Thompson, *The Dry Mock*.

KIERKEGAARD, S., *The Concept of Irony, with Constant Reference to Socrates*, 1841, trans. Lee M. Capel, London, 1966.

Rewarding for those who have some familiarity with the concepts of nineteenth-century German philosophy, difficult for those who have not.

PIRANDELLO, L., *On Humour*, 1920, ed. and tr. Antonio Illiano and D. P. Testa, Chapel Hill, 1975.

Pirandello's 'humour' is close to irony, particularly to what might be called the General Irony of inevitable self-deception.

THOMPSON, J. A. K., *Irony: An Historical Introduction*, London, 1926.

Deals only with Greek and Latin authors, including orators and historians.

CHEVALIER, H., *The Ironic Temper: Anatole France and his Time*, New York, 1932.

The second and sixth chapters discuss irony in general.

SEDGEWICK, G. G., *Of Irony, Especially in Drama*, 1935, 2nd ed., Toronto, 1948.

A valuable chapter on the history of the concept of irony, though misleading on Romantic Irony. Other chapters on 'Irony in Drama', 'The Clytemnestra plays', and *Othello*.

BIRNEY, E., 'English Irony Before Chaucer', *University of Toronto Quarterly*, VI (July, 1937), pp. 538–57.

Not adequate, however, on Dramatic Irony in Old English narrative poetry.

MANN, T., 'Die Kunst des Romans', 1939, trans. as 'The Art of The Novel' in *The Creative Vision*, eds. Haskell M. Block and Herman Salinger, New York, 1960.

On the relationship of irony and the 'epic' novel.

WORCESTER, D., *The Art of Satire*, Cambridge, Mass., 1940. Chapter IV, Irony, the Ally of Comedy; Chapter V, Irony, the Ally of Tragedy; Chapter VI, Section iv, Rebirth of Irony, Section v, Sphinxes without Secrets.

An eminently readable work.

THOMPSON, A. R., *The Dry Mock, A Study of Irony in Drama*, Berkeley, 1948.

Attempts a coherent theory of irony, but defines irony too exclusively. Principal ironists discussed: Tieck, Pirandello, Molière, Shaw, Aeschylus, Sophocles, Euripides, and Ibsen. An important work.

BROOKS, C., 'Irony and "Ironic" Poetry', *College English*, IX (1948), pp. 231–7, revised as 'Irony as a Principle of Structure' for *Literary Opinion in America*, ed. Morton Zabel, New York, 1951 (rev. ed.), pp. 729–41. See also Brooks's *The Well-Wrought Urn*, London, 1949.
An influential essay that extended (and weakened) the concept of irony. Criticized by R. S. Crane in 'The Critical Monism of Cleanth Brooks' in *Critics and Criticism*, ed. R. S. Crane, Chicago, 1952, pp. 83–107, and by William Righter in his *Logic and Criticism*, London, 1963.

WARREN, R. P., 'Pure and Impure Poetry' in *Critiques and Essays in Criticism*, ed. R. W. Stallman, New York, 1949.
An interesting elaboration of I. A. Richards's definition of irony as 'the bringing in of the opposite, the complementary impulses'.

WRIGHT, A. H., 'Irony and Fiction', *Journal of Aesthetics and Art Criticism*, XII (1953), pp. 111–18.
A useful brief summary stressing the importance of style. But it defines irony too exclusively.

WELLEK, R., *A History of Modern Criticism 1750–1950; II: The Romantic Age*, London, 1955.
Valuable for its account of the German theorists.

FRYE, N., *Anatomy of Criticism*, Princeton, 1957.
An attempt to relate irony to other kinds of writing and to define its place in the evolution of imaginative literature.

GUREWITCH, M. L., *European Romantic Irony*, Ph.D. dissertation (1957), Ann Arbor, 1962.
An interesting general introduction with discussions of Byron, Baudelaire, Büchner, Carlyle, Flaubert, Théophile Gautier, Heine, Leopardi, Alfred de Musset, and Stendhal.

WATT, I., 'The Ironic Tradition in Augustan Prose from Swift to Johnson', in *Restoration and Augustan Prose*, Los Angeles, 1957[?].
Some valuable observations on the relationship of irony and eighteenth-century prose.

SHARPE, R. B., *Irony in the Drama*, Chapel Hill, N.C., 1959.
More valuable on 'impersonation in drama' than on irony.

BOOTH, W. C., *The Rhetoric of Fiction*, Chicago, 1961.
An indispensable treatment of the dangers of irony in 'impersonal' and 'point-of-view' narrative methods.

KNOX, N., *The Word IRONY and Its Context, 1500–1755*, Durham, N.C., 1961.
A detailed, scholarly account of the development of the concept of irony within the period named.

HUTCHENS, E., *Irony in* TOM JONES, Alabama, 1965.
Has an introductory chapter on the nature of irony and an interesting classification of types of Verbal Irony.

GLICKSBERG, C. I., *The Ironic Vision in Modern Literature*, The Hague, 1969.
The first work to be devoted entirely to 'General Irony'. Discusses a wide range of European writers but tends to make them look too much the same.

MUECKE, D. C., *The Compass of Irony*, London, 1969.
Part I discusses the nature of irony and illustrates in some detail

the principal kinds. Part II deals chiefly with General and Romantic Irony and attempts to relate the development of these to developments in the history of European thought.

BOOTH, W. C., *A Rhetoric of Irony*, Chicago, 1974.
A clear account of the problems and pleasures of interpreting irony.

GENERAL WORKS IN OTHER LANGUAGES

JANCKE, R., *Das Wesen der Ironie: Strukturanalyse ihrer Erscheinungsformen*, Leipzig, 1929.

JANKÉLÉVITCH, V., *L'Ironie, ou La Bonne Conscience*, 1936, 2nd (revised) edn., Paris, 1950.
A brilliant, indeed a dazzling work at a very general level. Largely indebted to Kierkegaard. Reviewed by Wilson O. Clough, 'Irony: A French Approach', *Sewanee Review*, XLVII, 1939, pp. 175–83.

ALLEMANN, B., *Ironie und Dichtung*, Pfullingen, 1956.
On irony in German literature from Schlegel to Musil.

STROHSCHNEIDER-KOHRS, I., *Die romantische Ironie in Theorie und Gestaltung*, Tübingen, 1960.
The definitive study of Romantic Irony.

BEHLER, E., *Keassische Ironie, romantische Ironie, tragische Ironie. Zum Ursprung dieser Begriffe*. Darmstadt, 1972.

Index